EXPLOSIVE
Basketball Training

Michael Yessis, Ph.D.

COACHES CHOICE™

ISBN: 1-58518-659-7
Library of Congress Catalog Number: 2002104667
Cover design: Kerry Hartjen
Text design: Jeanne Hamilton

Coaches Choice
P.O. Box 1828
Monterey, CA 93942
www.coacheschoice.com

DEDICATION

This book is dedicated to all aspiring basketball players, regardless of age or level of playing ability. If you want to improve, this book is for you. It can help you develop the ability to reach your full potential and to get the greatest enjoyment from this great sport.

ACKNOWLEDGMENTS

I am deeply indebted to many people who have helped make this book possible. Without their assistance and sometimes perseverance, this book would not have its many unique and informational features. Each person played a very important role, thus the order in which their names appear is not related to the value of their contribution. More specifically, I would like to thank the following:

Robert Dye, one of the models for execution of the key basketball skills and some of the exercises. He now plays for the Gary Steelheads of the CBA.

Cliff Harski, a player at Ramona High School who now plays on a collegiate level. He was a model for the basketball skills and exercises.

Kyle Truesdale, a model for basketball skills and special exercises. He was a player on the Ramona High School basketball team.

Michael Rivera, a model for some of the basketball skills. He was a player on the Ramona High School basketball team.

Yosef Johnson, a trainer/manager, for his assistance in putting me in contact with Robert Dye.

Al Schaffer, coach of the Ramona basketball team during the 2000-01 season, for his assistance in selecting the players and making arrangements for the filming.

Marissa Yessis for her assistance in importing, capturing, and organizing the digital pictures used in this book.

Dr. Tobin Watkinson, a renowned clinical nutritionist, chiropractor, and good friend, for his assistance in preparing the chapter on nutrition.

Edie Yessis, my lovely wife, for her patience and understanding during the course of working on this book.

CONTENTS

Making a Hard Game Easy

Through decades of helping elite-level athletes maximize their performance, I have concluded that simply *playing* any given sport is easy. Reaching the highest level of competition – now *that's* the tough part. It takes physical skill, hard work, and no small amount of luck for any athlete to reach the highest level of his chosen sport. I can't help with the luck or the work ethic. But as someone who has devoted his entire adult life to the science of athletic performance, I can help athletes at all levels enhance the specific technical and physical skills needed for virtually any sport.

This book is about basketball, and it includes many of the physical qualities it takes to excel on the court. To the casual observer, playing basketball looks easy. All you have to do is run, jump, and shoot the ball through a hoop – child's play. Now, if you're a serious player, coach or trainer, you're laughing at this comment. You know basketball is a complex and physically demanding sport. Before even looking at the basket, players must get into position to take and make (or deny opponents') shots. This requires strategy, teamwork, and a specific set of physical and technical skills.

So what do aspiring basketball players do? Most spend more time playing, buying different equipment (especially shoes), and seeking out better coaching. Unusually gifted individuals – with 36-inch vertical leaps, speed, agility, strength, and flexibility – make it look easy. However, the vast majority of athletes don't possess these skills naturally. To compete with and ultimately defeat the so-called *naturals*, they must develop physical skills and their skill technique through a combination of *hard* and *smart* work.

The most important thing to understand is that athletes (in this case, basketball players) can improve their speed and quickness, and reduce likelihood of injury, through the principles included in this book. It's not extraordinarily difficult to perfect technique and develop physical abilities as they relate to execution of these skills. By developing physical abilities in the same basic patterns of movements exhibited by athletes at the highest level, aspiring athletes will achieve their genetic potential.

Doing special exercises designed to improve strength, flexibility, and the speed of movement and technique, improves athletes' playing ability beyond their wildest expectations. I have seen thousands of athletes significantly improve their speed, agility, jumping, and shooting by making simple changes in their technique and improving their basketball-specific physical abilities.

But there's more – *much more*. By modifying technique and doing special strength, flexibility, and explosive exercises, athletes who experience back and hamstring problems find that their pain disappears. Others find it easier to concentrate on complex strategy once they've improved their physical skills and confidence. These players develop greater control and feel for the muscle actions used in executing the various movements and skills inherent in basketball. Every player can experience improvement in his game. When the physical training to improve strength and flexibility is coupled with speed and explosive training, the results are even more impressive.

For the athlete, learning and applying the techniques described in this book may be the first step to getting the fullest possible enjoyment and satisfaction from playing basketball. Athletes, coaches, and trainers will be amazed by how much progress is possible in a relatively short time. This applies not only to making changes in skill techniques, but also to specific physical abilities, problems and injuries.

Although basketball is a team sport, each position requires a specific set of physical and technical skills. Each athlete brings a unique set of physical and mental abilities to the table. Regardless of how they run, cut, jump, and shoot, athletes must execute specific skill actions in order to play successfully. How well they execute these actions depends on their physical abilities. More specifically, their physical abilities determine: how much they rely on each joint action, the range of motion of each action, and the force involved in each action in the execution of key skills.

The concept of biomechanical analysis is central to my programs. A biomechanical analysis answers such questions as: Is the specific physical action effective? If so, why is it effective? What is the role of each joint action? Which joint actions may be changed to make the technique more effective? How may the specific actions be made more powerful? Should the technique be modified? And if so, how? Most standard instruction does not address these points.

By applying the laws of biomechanics and kinesiology, it's possible to provide accurate descriptions of what takes place during the execution of each of the skills involved in basketball, including the critical role each joint action plays. To determine the key actions involved in running, cutting, jumping, and shooting, I biomechanically

analyzed many of the best players in the world to determine and evaluate which actions are used and the sequence of their occurrence. I used high-speed videotaping and frame-by-frame analysis of the tapes to identify key joint actions in execution of each of these various skills. I selected photos to identify and illustrate these major actions, and created special strength, flexibility, and explosive exercises to duplicate these actions. The strength, flexibility, and explosiveness gained by doing these exercises have an immediate and positive impact on the athlete's play.

By examining each key action, you will gain a better understanding of each skill and how specialized flexibility, strength, and explosive exercises can improve each joint action and resultant performance. This knowledge and its application to skill improvement speeds progress rapidly. By studying illustrations of these actions, and doing the specialized exercises that duplicate the actions in each of these skills, athletes gain a better understanding of how each of the exercises relates to personal playing and abilities.

Although this book contains a great deal of information, I have made a serious attempt to present it in a simple and straightforward manner. It is well illustrated with actual sequence pictures of players executing the various skills, and with the exercises that are specific to the main actions involved in each of the key basketball skills. You should not think of it as a book on conditioning for basketball. Rather, you should approach it as something that will give you a much better understanding of basketball skills, and how you can improve athletic performance in the shortest amount of time. If you follow the program outlined here, I guarantee outstanding results.

CHAPTER 1

General Versus Specialized Conditioning

Being in top physical condition enables an athlete to play an entire game without undue fatigue, while executing various skills at the highest level and incurring fewer injuries. However, general conditioning has its limitations. Yes, high-school-aged athletes, whose bodies are still maturing, will see changes in their abilities to shoot, run, and cut. General conditioning programs, combined with physical maturation processes, enable these younger athletes to play on a higher level.

The visible benefits of general conditioning programs clearly subside once an athlete reaches college age. At this time, a general conditioning program merely allows the athlete to maintain the previous year's level of play. While there may be a slight improvement, the athlete's overall pattern of play is basically the same.

If you want to play better, outrun opponents, jump higher, shoot more three-pointers, and elude or stay with opponents, you will need a specialized exercise program. Being able to execute the skills more effectively will get you greater enjoyment from the game.

But what about those athletes who play for something more? This could be you, someone you know, or someone you coach. While we like to think that all athletes ultimately play for enjoyment, that enjoyment often derives from winning, becoming a celebrity, earning a handsome living, having one's college education paid through an athletics-based grant-in-aid, achieving all-star status, or making a competitive high school or club team. The key word is *competitive*. When you play sports at the highest level, it's all about competition and gaining the competitive edge. To achieve success, athletes know they need something more than general physical conditioning. They need the kind of specialized training that duplicates sport-specific movements and actions. They need what's in this book. To understand the concept of specialized conditioning, you should have a basic understanding of its counterpart, general conditioning.

General Conditioning

General strength exercises condition the overall body. They are not related to the specific actions seen in executing such basic basketball skills as running, cutting, shooting, and jumping. General exercises do not strengthen muscles as they are used in execution of these skills, nor do they increase an athlete's functional potential to better these skills.

The crunch exercise illustrates this concept nicely. The crunch is a common exercise used in fitness programs. You lie on your back and raise your head and shoulders off the floor. The legs are usually bent and placed up on a chair, or the feet may remain in contact with the ground.

This exercise is very effective for strengthening the upper portion of the abdominal muscles. However, execution of certain basketball skills only minimally involves the upper abdominals. Much more important are the lower abdominals and the oblique muscles, located on the sides of the abdomen. These muscles are crucial to running and cutting, and many of the twisting and rotational actions employed in passing and eluding a defender.

Thus, the crunch is a good exercise for strengthening the upper portion of the abdominals, but not directly related to execution of basketball skills. But that doesn't make it useless. If you have weak abdominals, the crunch may indirectly help strengthen your trunk muscles and improve other skills. However, because it does not duplicate the trunk movements in the exact actions (pathways) seen in execution of specific basketball skills, it does little if anything to improve an athlete's running, quickness, jumping, and shooting.

The key to improving athletic performance is doing specialized exercises that duplicate the movements and actions seen in actual competitive skills. In this way, by developing basketball-specific strengths and skills, athletes can achieve quantum gains in playing performance.

Specialized Conditioning

Specialized strength exercises develop the physical and psychological qualities that apply directly to basketball. These exercises are designed and selected so that the movement and actions they enhance closely match those seen in the execution of various basketball skills.

Specialized exercises that promote positive psychological traits consist of movements and actions that require decisiveness, willpower, perseverance, and confidence. They promote the kind of *mental toughness* that leads to success on the court.

Execution of certain specialized exercises requires concentration to develop a specific neuromuscular pathway. Take for example a strength exercise that duplicates one aspect of a jump shot – it takes ultimate concentration and perseverance to repeat exactly the same movement time after time. For specialized exercises to have maximum positive transfer, the athlete must be decisive in his movements and actions. This promotes the kind of confidence that takes over and wins games in high-pressure situations.

Criteria for Specialized Strength Exercises

For an exercise to be specific it must fulfill one or more of the following criteria:

- The exercise must duplicate the exact movement witnessed in certain actions of the particular skill. For example, exercises that duplicate a specific action in shooting, an action in the knee joint in jumping, an action in the trunk when passing, an action in the hip joint when running, and so on.

- The exercise must involve the same type of muscular contraction as used in execution of the skill. For example, in the jump shot, the knee-joint extensor muscles (quadriceps) undergo an explosive-shortening contraction (after being pre-tensed) to produce maximal force and resultant jump height. After the initial explosive contraction, the limbs continue to straighten on their own momentum until the legs are straight or the antagonist muscles undergo a strong-lengthening (eccentric) contraction to slow down and stop the limbs before an injury occurs. The specialized strength exercise must include an explosive-muscular contraction as occurs in the knee-joint action.

- The specialized exercise must have the same range of motion as in the actual competitive skill. For example, in doing the lunge exercise as done in bodybuilding, you take a very short forward step, and then squat. A more accurate term for this exercise may be a split-squat. However, when reaching for a loose ball, or trying to steal the ball, or attempting to get by an opponent, the first step is usually long. Thus, it's necessary to do a classical lunge, stepping out as far as possible before lowering the body. This is more specific to the execution of game skills, as it duplicates the exact range of motion in which strength is applied.

A New Concept

The concept of exercise specificity is new to basketball. The term *specificity* is not. Many authors have used the term *specific exercises*, but few exercises actually fulfill the above criteria. The specificity referred to by these authors usually refers to strengthening or stretching the muscles that may be involved, but not necessarily in the way they are used in executing basketball skills.

Running the steps in the basketball arena to develop strength of the legs is a classic example of a general exercise that is not specific to running. Raising the thighs and pushing off when the thigh is perpendicular to the trunk is not in the same range of action and omits the important initial explosive contraction of the hip flexors required to drive the thigh forward to increase running speed.

Its value lies in ankle-joint extension, which drives the body upward rather than forward, as is needed in running. This ankle action is beneficial.

But because of the need to drive the knees up – not forward – it plays a secondary role in improving jump height and running speed.

Typical strength and conditioning programs for basketball players offer general exercises to get players in shape. In some cases, the prescribed exercises use the same muscles as are used in running, cutting, shooting, and jumping. But if these exercises do not duplicate the exact range of motion, the same type of muscular contraction, or the exact movement and coordination as seen in execution of these skills, they will not be functional; they will not directly improve the athlete's ability to execute these skills.

For maximum effectiveness, the development of strength must be synchronized with basketball playing. This is considered usable strength; the strength gained that can be displayed in playing the sport. This is the greatest value of specialized exercises.

Because of the need for skill duplication, most exercises—especially those that focus on leg, hip, and shoulder actions—are best done with elastic tubing, such as the Active Cords set developed by the author. This unique set consists of three different tension elastic cords that can be used separately or in combination, a non-slip hip belt, an ankle strap, two handles, and a dual attachment strap to fit in a door, a beam, or a post. With this equipment, you can do individual arm and leg actions, and hip and shoulder rotational and linear movements. The reason for this is that it is difficult—and in some cases impossible—to duplicate the exact movements of the legs, hips, and shoulders with barbells or machines. Medicine ball and dumbbell exercises are also important.

CHAPTER 2

Active Versus Static Stretching

Much of what you'll find in this book challenges long-held, cherished notions regarding appropriate strength and conditioning training for basketball. Chapter 1 suggests that when it comes to basketball, true specialized conditioning is more effective than its more traditional general conditioning counterpart in developing key physical skills. In this chapter, it's recommended to have a program of active stretching, as opposed to static stretching, as one building block for the kind of flexibility needed for *Explosive Basketball* training and play. The following are some definitions and descriptions.

Static Stretching

In static stretching, the athlete holds a particular position for up to 30 (or more) seconds to stretch the muscles and connective tissue surrounding the joint being worked. For example, basketball players often lean into a wall to stretch the Achilles tendon and calf muscles, or bend over to touch the toes to stretch the hamstrings. The key to successful execution of these stretches is to hold the position while relaxing the muscles as much as possible, providing a gradual increase in range of motion (ROM). These static stretches require muscle relaxation to counteract the muscle and tendon reflexes, which tend to hold back increases in ROM.

Here's the fundamental problem: basketball is a very dynamic sport that requires active and forceful movements of the legs and arms, especially in running, cutting, jumping, and rebounding. The joint actions are ballistic in nature; they are initiated with a strong muscular contraction to accelerate the limb and place it in motion, after which it continues on its own momentum. The movement is stopped by contraction of antagonist muscles. Such ballistic movements create great forces. The body must deal with these forces to absorb (dampen) them and, most importantly, to accumulate energy for giveback in a push-off or return action.

By its very nature, static stretching exerts insignificant force (aside from possible compression forces in the joints involved). During the static stretch, muscles are completely relaxed, whereas in playing, muscles perform actively with dynamic concentric and eccentric contractions. The forces experienced in such movements far surpass those experienced in static stretching. As a result, static stretching doesn't prepare basketball players for the type of forceful movements inherent in the game, and injuries can result. Recent studies show that static stretches done prior to playing do not decrease the number of injuries experienced. To the contrary, they may actually contribute to some injuries.

Static stretching also limits the nervous system's vital role in activating muscles to insure adequate stretching. This concept requires some explanation. If you have a flexibility range of 180 degrees during the more demanding moments in a game, but your muscles are only strong enough to move a limb voluntarily through 150 degrees, you won't work the remaining 30 degrees during static stretching. Static stretching doesn't activate muscles as they're activated when executing many of the specific skills and movements typical of basketball. This occurs only when you involve both the muscles and the corresponding nerves that send the signals to the muscles for a timely, correctly intense contraction. Static stretching effectively minimizes the role of the nervous system (and the stretch's basketball-specific effect).

The main outcome of prolonged static stretching is permanent elongation of the tissues. Excessive stretching may stretch the ligaments and other tissues to such a degree that they lose elasticity. The problem is compounded if no supplementary strength training is done to maintain the integrity of the joint. This is one reason why there are so many injuries in basketball, especially to the lower back. Static stretching also includes contraindicated stretching – the straight-leg, seated, and bent-over toe touch. Eliminate these common (and dangerous) stretches from your workout.

Active Stretching

Unlike its static counterpart, active stretching simultaneously stretches and strengthens joint-support structures through the full ROM typical of movements experienced in an actual game. Active stretching is a true warm-up; it literally raises the temperature of the muscle prior to participation. By doing active stretches with involvement of the muscles and joints through a full ROM, the muscles warm up and become prepared for the activity.

Full-range exercises against resistance offer the greatest functional increase in ROM. When stretches are accompanied by strengthening, the danger of injury decreases tremendously. The muscles and joints are truly ready for activity.

Active stretches with resistance yield strength and flexibility through the full ROM. This reduces the amount of time needed for such training and assures greater benefit from the work being done. When active stretches are done, the newly created ROM is functional, which means it will be involved in execution of the basic skills.

There are many forms of active stretches, ranging from relatively simple stretches to complex, explosive-type stretches. In all cases, active stretches involve muscular work during the stretch. This ensures maximum joint safety and prepares muscles for the forthcoming action. Active stretches can involve contraction of muscles to perform a movement that stretches the antagonist muscles, or use gravity to provide the force to go through the ROM.

The major muscular contraction involved in active stretches is the eccentric contraction. The muscle develops tension while its overall length increases; it stretches under tension. For example, when you experience touchdown during running, there is slight flexion in the ankle, knee, and hip joints to absorb and withstand the landing forces. As soon as the feet touch the ground, the muscles and tendons immediately tense. In many cases, this actually occurs prior to contact, to handle the forces and accumulate energy for pushing off again.

When you push off, the muscles shorten; they contract concentrically. In this situation (when gravity is the force pulling you down) the same muscles are involved in the down phase (landing – eccentric contraction) as in the up phase (push off – concentric contraction).

When a muscle or muscle group initiates a movement (for example, the thigh drive in running), the muscles work in unison. The agonist muscles initiate the action. The antagonist muscles limit and stop the action. The hip flexors contract (shorten) to drive the thigh forward, and the hamstrings contract eccentrically (lengthen) to limit hip flexion and prevent injury.

Instead of thinking in terms of the muscles that need stretching, think in terms of muscle and joint actions. Doing this provides a better understanding of how stretches relate to the key joint actions that occur, and how they not only prepare the athlete for execution of skills, but can also improve overall playing ability.

Another way of looking at functional ROM is to equate the stretch with exactly what takes place in the joint. Does the stretch duplicate what takes place in the joint in relation to the ROM? Does the stretch duplicate the type of muscular contraction that is elicited during an active action?

Studies have shown that the landing forces in jumping can be 10 or more times an athlete's body weight, depending on jump height and how he lands. Muscles and joints must be able to handle these great (anticipated) forces. The joints and their associated tissues also must be able to cope with unexpected, irregular and sudden loads, as when landing on uneven surfaces (such as on someone's foot) or being hit by another player.

Stretches for Specific Joint Actions

It is highly recommended that the following stretches be a part of any player's workout and preparation routine. Each stretch or group of stretches works the joint and its supporting structures, effectively increasing usable range of motion and reducing likelihood of injury.

Ankle (Foot) Flexion and Extension

Ankle (foot) flexion occurs in the landing and extension in the takeoff when running, cutting and jumping. The landing and takeoff are controlled to a great extent by the muscles and support structures of the foot (mainly the arch) and the muscles that act on the ankle. The gastrocnemius muscle and Achilles tendon are especially important in ankle extension when speed and force are increased. The soleus muscle, which also extends the ankle, is active at all speeds, but especially in relatively slow movements and for prolonged periods of playing.

On a ball-heel, or mid-foot landing, it is important to have eccentric strength and flexibility of the ankle extensor muscles and tendons, i.e., the Achilles tendon, the gastrocnemius and soleus, and the support structures of the arch. In the takeoff, foot (ankle) extension (concentric contraction) takes place, which involves the calf muscles and tendons. The ankle action should be full range. An upward rebound of the arch contributes to running speed and jump height. The best stretches to improve the ROM in this action are standing ankle extensions.

The Wall Stretch

Stand with one foot flat on the floor, two to four feet away from a wall. Place hands against the wall approximately shoulder high. Stand far enough away from the wall to feel the stretch when your heel is on the floor. You should feel a strong eccentric stretch of the tendons and muscles. Hold the position for one to two seconds, then rise up on the ball of the foot and hold the up position for two seconds. Lower the heel at a moderate rate of speed until you feel the stretch when the heel is down. Hold momentarily and repeat by rising up on the ball of the foot and holding. Holding in the top position is important for concentration on full ankle-joint extension during the push-off (Figures 2-1a and 2-1b). Execution on both legs is also effective (Figure 2-1c).

Leg (Knee) Flexion and Extension

Basketball players don't need a great range of flexion-extension motion in the knee joint. The joint undergoes flexion (eccentric stretch) on jumping, cutting, and running landings. But with ample eccentric strength, the less the bend, the more effective the action. Achieving a 90- to 110-degree ROM in the knee joint is usually more than sufficient to stretch the muscles involved and prepare for play.

The Squat Stretch

This stretches the anterior thigh muscles (quadriceps). Stand with feet hip-width apart, feet flat on the floor, with trunk erect. Lock the lower back in its normal curvature (slightly arched lumbar spine) and slowly go into a squat. The hips should move to the rear and the trunk should incline forward while the spine remains stable. Lower the body (think of lowering the hips) while holding the normal curvature of the spine at all times. Stop at or before the thigh-parallel position, or when there is less than a 90-degree angle between the back of the thigh and shin. Rise up, relax, and repeat. Be sure that the heels stay in contact with the ground. This provides an Achilles-tendon stretch and ensures that the knees stay over the feet when lowering the body. This prevents knee injury (Figures 2-2a and 2-2b).

Figure 2-1a

Figure 2-1b

Figure 2-1c

Hip Flexion and Extension

Hip flexion and extension play key roles in running and cutting. These actions control stride length, effectiveness of all push-offs, and running speed. It's important to have ample flexibility in the hip joints. Hip flexibility increases stride length and how far the athlete can step out when trying to steal or reach a ball. Hip-extensor flexibility also determines how high the thigh can be raised or how low you can bend over for the hips when reaching forward.

Hip Flexion

The hip-joint flexor and adductor muscles are strongly involved in running and cutting as they pull the thigh forward. The adductors initiate the hip flexion, and then allow the stronger hip flexors to take over when they are in better position. To stretch the hip flexors, do the lunge. To isolate the hip joint adductor muscles, do the side lunge, also known as the groin stretch.

Figure 2-2a

Figure 2-2b

Figure 2-3a

Figure 2-3b

The Lunge

Assume a standing position with the feet hip-width apart. Take a very long forward step and plant the foot with the toes facing forward. Keep the trunk erect and slowly lower the body (eccentric stretch). Keep the rear leg straight but relaxed, and the toes in line with the leg. As more weight falls on the front leg, a strong stretch of the hip flexors results. Hold the down position for one to two seconds, and then push off with the forward leg to resume the initial standing position. Repeat with the opposite leg. Be sure to keep the torso erect and the rear leg straight but relaxed. Leaning forward or bending the rear leg reduces the stretch's effectiveness (Figures 2-3a and 2-3b).

Hip Extension

The hip extensors must be actively stretched to prepare them for pulling the leg back and down to make contact with the floor in running and cutting actions. These muscles also play a role in relation to how far the swing-leg thigh can be driven forward during the push-off in running or in stepping out (reaching forward) without adversely rotating the hips. The hip extensors (the gluteus maximus and hamstring muscles) can be actively stretched in two ways: one, with active participation of the hip flexors, and two, with no participation of the hip flexors.

Lying Leg Raises

To do a stretch with active involvement of the hip flexors, assume a prone position, face-up, with the arms alongside the body and the legs out straight. When ready, hold one leg straight and raise it up as high as possible, but not past the vertical position. Lower to the floor and raise up again in a continuous action. When the leg is raised via the concentric contraction of the hip flexors, the hip extensors undergo an eccentric stretch. With every leg raise, you should be able to go a little further in your ROM. After doing the stretch with one leg, repeat with the other. You may alternate the legs during execution (Figures 2-4a and 2-4b).

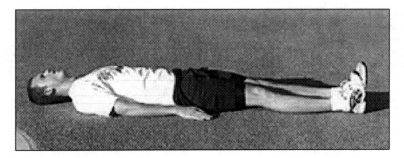

Figure 2-4a

Figure 2-4b

The Good Morning

This active stretch does not involve the hip flexors and uses gravity as the moving force, isolating the action to the hamstrings. (The gluteus maximus is also involved if you go through a sufficiently great ROM.) To execute, assume a standing position with the feet hip-width apart. When ready, contract the lower back muscles to lock the lumbar spine in its normal, slightly arched curvature. Hold the spine rigid and the legs straight. Bend forward from the hips until you feel a strong stretch of the hamstrings. Push the hips back as you bend forward (Figures 2-5a and 2-5b).

For most athletes, the incline is approximately 30 to 45 degrees forward. Be sure to maintain the normal curvature of the spine as you feel the eccentric stretch of the hamstring muscles and tendons. Hold for one to two seconds. Rise up by contracting the hamstrings concentrically. Relax before repeating. Try to achieve slightly greater ROM on each bend.

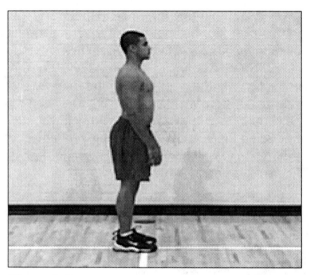

Figure 2-5a

Figure 2-5b

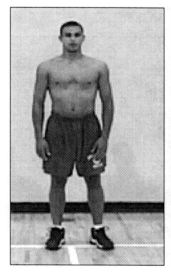

Figure 2-6a   **Figure 2-6b**   **Figure 2-6c**

Hip Adduction and Abduction

The ability to move laterally is extremely important in basketball. This demands a full ROM for lateral movement in the hip joint and adequate strength of the hip-joint abductor muscles to allow for forceful and powerful lateral or sideward actions. This is the key to cutting, reacting to an opponent's changes in direction, and for getting free from an opponent. Having adequate levels of strength and flexibility of the adductor muscles helps prevent groin injuries, which typically occur when taking a quick and long sideward step. The side lunge stretches the adductor muscles.

The Side Lunge

Assume a standing position with the feet shoulder-width apart and arms alongside the body. Take a long step directly out to the side and plant the foot at a 45-degree angle to the outside. Keep the torso erect. Slowly lower the body so that its weight is concentrated on the forward leg, while keeping the rear (push-off) leg straight. You will feel the stretch in the groin almost immediately. Hold the bottom position for one to two seconds. Rise up and repeat with the other leg (Figures 2-6a and 2-6b). Be sure to keep the trunk erect at all times. To do this, keep the arms overhead (Figure 2-6c).

Hip-Joint Abduction

To stretch the muscles on the outside of the hip joint, do the side bend described later in this chapter.

Shoulder-Joint (Arm) Flexion and Abduction

The ROM in the shoulder joint is important in many basketball skills. Arm flexion and abduction actions determine the athlete's ability to raise the arms overhead and to reach far in front and out to the side in all directions. These arm actions are important for catching overhead passes, stealing the ball, shooting, rebounding, and blocking shots.

Most athletes have ample flexibility in the shoulder joint to raise their arms shoulder-level or higher. But many have only limited ability to raise their arms high overhead. Most stretching should be done to raise the arm completely upward, ensuring a full ROM for shooting over an opponent, reaching high passes, blocking shots, and rebounding.

Front-Arm Raises

Assume a standing position with the arms alongside the body. When ready, keep the arms straight and raise them directly in front completely overhead. In

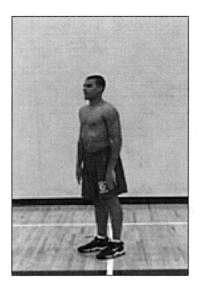

Figure 2-7a

Figure 2-7b

Figure 2-7c

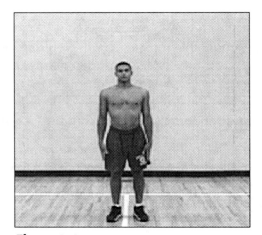

Figure 2-8a

Figure 2-8b

Figure 2-8c

Figure 2-8d

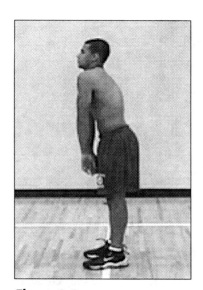

Figure 2-9a

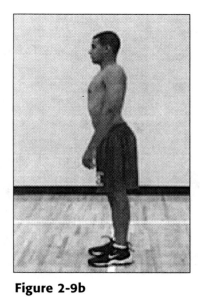

Figure 2-9b

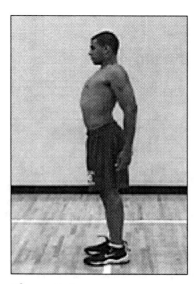

Figure 2-9c

the ending position, the arms should be directly overhead. The entire body should be fully extended with slightly more hyperextension in the lumbar spine. The arms should be alongside the head, obscuring a side view of the ears.

Raise and lower the arms in a repetitive manner, trying to increase the ROM on the up phase of each repetition. Raise and lower until achieving the highest position possible (Figures 2-7a through 2-7c). In this stretch, you also have maximum elevation of the shoulders.

Lateral-Arm Raises

Assume a standing position with the arms alongside the body. When ready, keep the arms straight and raise them out to the side and up as high as possible overhead. In the ending position, the arms should be straight, pointed directly upward, with the body should be fully extended. Again, the arms should obscure a side view of the ears.

Raise and lower the arms at a moderate rate of speed, trying to increase the ROM on the up phase

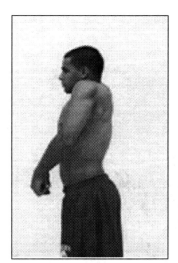
Figure 2-10a

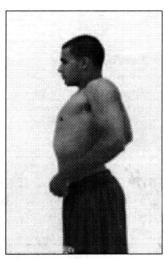
Figure 2-10b

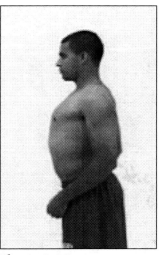
Figure 2-10c

Figure 2-10d

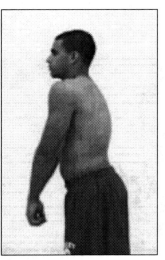
Figure 2-10e

of each repetition. When you're able to clap hands directly overhead with the arms straight, you have achieved the maximum ROM needed in the shoulder joint (Figures 2-8a through 2-8d). This stretch also gives maximum elevation of the shoulders.

Protraction-Retraction

To maximize forward and backward reach, the athlete must loosen up his or her shoulders, or more specifically, the shoulder girdle, i.e., the movement of the scapulae. To execute, assume a comfortable standing position with arms alongside the body. When ready, move the shoulders as far forward as possible (protraction). In essence, give yourself the appearance of a sunken chest. After reaching the most forward position, bring the shoulders as far back as possible (retraction), sticking out the chest. Limit the action to shoulder movement forward and backward. The arms should remain hanging at the sides and be loose at all times (Figures 2-9a through 2-9c).

Shoulder Circles

This stretch loosens up the shoulder in all directions. For a full ROM of the arm, the athlete must have

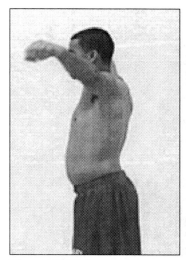

Figure 2-11a

Figure 2-11b

Figure 2-11c

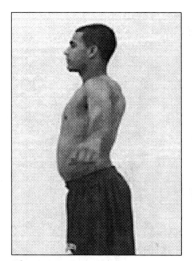

Figure 2-11d

Figure 2-11e

Figure 2-11f

Figure 2-12a

Figure 2-12b

Figure 2-12c

loose shoulders. This adds considerably to the distance the arms can move. To execute, assume a comfortable standing position with arms alongside the body. When ready, elevate the shoulders as high as possible. Rotate the shoulders to the rear, down and forward, as far as possible. Continue upward until completing the circle. Repeat (Figures 2-10a through 2-10e).

Arm Circles

Arm circles are basically the same as shoulder circles, with the addition of arm movement. To execute, assume a comfortable standing position with arms out to the side in line with the shoulders. The body and arms form the letter T. When ready, raise the arms upward and backward, then downward and forward, followed by an upward and backward motion. Round the corners as you move upward-backward-downward-forward so that the hands circumscribe a circle when viewed from the side. Start off with relatively small circles. Gradually increase the size for greater flexibility and a greater stretch of the shoulder joint and shoulder girdle. If you have relatively loose shoulders, it's not necessary to do shoulder circles, as arm circles are similar but offer a greater ROM (Figures 2-11a through 2-11f).

Overhead Reach with a Side Bend

The Overhead Reach is used a great deal when leaping for rebounds or for a tip-in. The key is to have maximum flexibility in the shoulder joint and to

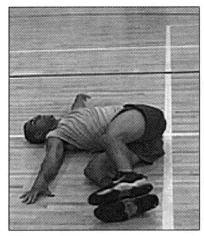
Figure 2-13a

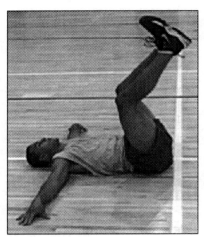
Figure 2-13b

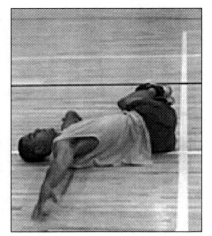
Figure 2-13c

be able to bend the body sideways, creating greater effective height. This stretch combines an overhead reach and a side bend.

To execute, assume a comfortable standing position. Raise one arm as high as possible. Elevate the shoulder completely. After reaching as high as possible, bend the body sideways to reach even higher (Figures 2-12a through 2-12c). Repeat with the other arm. For more flexibility in the waist, see side bends (Figures 2-14a through 2-14c) and side bends with a hip slide (Figures 2-15a through 2-15c) later in this chapter.

Midsection Bending and Rotation

The midsection is important in executing of many different actions common to basketball. Most important is rotation of the shoulders, which is needed in passing to the sides and receiving of the ball from sideward directions. It's also used when executing a sharp cut. Athletes bend sideways when reaching for a ball overhead or in front and to the side.

Reverse-Trunk Twist

For rotational-midsection actions and strengthening the specific muscles involved in that action, it's recommended to use the reverse-trunk twist. To execute, lie face-up on the floor with arms extended outward, perpendicular to the body. Bring the knees up so that the thighs are perpendicular to the trunk and the feet are off the floor. Keep the knees fully bent. When in position, lower the legs to one side until the knees touch the floor, or until reaching a point where you cannot go any further. The arms and shoulders maintain contact with the floor at all times. The thighs remain perpendicular to the trunk with the knees together.

Upon reaching the lowermost position, raise the thighs up and over to the other side as far as possible. Hold the bottom position for one to two seconds, then raise the thighs up and over to the other side. Repeat in a continuous manner until fully stretched. You should be able to lower the legs slightly more on each repetition.

When this exercise becomes easy, execute with straighter legs, but do not completely straighten the legs. When the legs are straightened, you should make contact with the foot instead of the knee. The straighter the legs are, the more difficult the exercise will be (Figures 2-13a through 2-13c).

Side Bends

Side bends promote lateral flexibility and strength of the midsection. To execute, assume a standing position with arms directly overhead and thumbs intertwined. Keep the arms straight. When you ready, lower the upper body to one side as far as possible while keeping the hips in position. Raise

Figure 2-14a

Figure 2-14b

Figure 2-14c

and lower the upper body to the opposite side while the hips remain in position. Repeat in a rhythmic manner, making sure the trunk remains erect (Figures 2-14a through 2-14c).

Side Bends with a Hip Slide

Execute side bends as illustrated in Figure 2-14, but include the hips in the stretch. To execute, slide the hips out to the opposite side while lowering the shoulders to one side. This increases the ROM and gives a full stretch on that entire side. Lower and rise from side to side in a steady continuous manner until fully stretched (Figures 2-15a through 2-15b).

Jogging and Easy Jumping

Jogging and easy jumping are not specific stretches, but are excellent activities to warm up the muscles in preparation for playing. By jogging, I mean running slowly. A short jog can precede the stretches, if desired. Easy jumping should follow jogging. Resume jogging with a gradual build-up in speed. Include cutting activities at this time, if desired

Figure 2-15a

Figure 2-15b

CHAPTER 3

Improving Jump Height

The ability to jump is one key predictor of basketball success. The higher and more quickly you can jump, the more successful you can be playing the game. Jumping affects many aspects of play, including shooting, rebounding, and shot blocking. This is why so many basketball players try every way possible to improve their jumping ability.

However, there is no magic formula to improve jumping ability. Some players possess a predominance of explosive white-muscle (fast-twitch) fibers. These are the so-called *natural* jumpers. Others have a predominance of red-muscle (slow-twitch) fibers. They have endurance and staying power. A player with more white fibers may fatigue more quickly and not be able to perform as well at the end of a game.

The percentage of *natural* jumpers is extremely small. More than 90% of all players have an equal distribution of muscle fibers. This means they can gain an advantage on most players *if they train properly*.

This can be done two ways: one is to improve technique, and the other is to develop the physical abilities specific to jumping. These include strength, speed-strength, explosiveness (power), and strength-endurance.

Improving technique and physical ability results in surprising gains—12 inches or more—especially for those who haven't previously trained specifically to improve this most important skill. As a bonus, improving technique and physical ability for jumping also results in increased speed and maneuverability. This is because the leg actions seen in jumping are also used in running, cutting, and overall court movement. So the potential for improving many aspects of a player's game is tremendous.

Jump Technique

The Biomechanics and Kinesiology of Jumping

The basic jump technique is the same regardless of the type of jump being executed. This means that the joint actions and the muscles involved in jumping are the same regardless of the jump or shot being executed.

Differences in jumping are found in the joint range of motion, the set-up for the shot, the type of approach, whether you are standing or moving, the speed of execution, and whether you are using one or both legs. The lay-up differs from the stationary (or spot-up) jump shot, which differs from a jump shot on the move. But in each case, the same leg actions are used in the takeoff.

Frame 1

Frame 2

Frame 3

Frame 4

Frame 5

Frame 6

Frame 7

Frame 8

Frame 9

Frame 10

Frame 11

Frame 12

Figure 3-1

Muscle Functions and Why They Are Important

To understand how you jump and why the different joint actions are necessary, it is important to understand what happens to the muscles during the jump. The changes, in regard to the type and intensity of the muscle contractions and the actions occurring in each joint movement, determine the height and speed of the jump. Knowing this helps you develop a better training program. It's important to first understand the three types of muscular contractions involved in jumping: *eccentric*, *isometric*, and *concentric*.

In the *eccentric* contraction, the muscle stretches and lengthens as it contracts and develops tension. This type of muscular contraction is used in all stopping and preparatory actions. The greater the tension developed in the muscle stretch, the stronger the muscular contraction.

The eccentric contraction occurs during a jump landing or preparatory (crouch) phase prior to executing a jump takeoff. For example, in the approach for a jump or a jump shot, you stop your forward progress by planting one and then the other foot about shoulder width apart. You bend in the ankles, knees, and hips; that is, you go into a slight crouch in preparation for the jump (Figure 3-1, frames 2 through 5; Figure 3-2, frames 1 and 2; Figure 3-3, frames 1 through 4). The down (crouching) movement is controlled by the eccentric contraction of the muscles involved in each joint action. This includes the calf muscles (the soleus and gastrocnemius), which are located on the upper part of the back of the shin. Together with the Achilles tendon, they increase in tension as they lengthen during the ankle flexion. In the knee joint, the quadriceps muscle of the anterior thigh develops great tension to stop you from going too low. In the hip joint, the hamstrings (back of thigh) and gluteus maximus (buttocks) undergo tension to limit how far you bend the trunk. The erector spinae muscles of the lumbar spine may also be involved to prevent excessive rounding of the lower back.

Frame 1

Frame 2

Frame 3

Frame 4

Frame 5

Frame 6

Figure 3-2

It's important to understand that, as the muscles lengthen and the tension becomes sufficiently great, the down (crouch) movement stops. The tension developed in the eccentric contraction limits the downward movement. It also prepares the muscles for the powerful shortening (concentric) contraction needed to jump upward. Muscle and tendon tension accumulates as a form of energy that can be returned in the takeoff.

In the lowermost portion of the crouch, immediately prior to takeoff, muscle contraction switches momentarily to *isometric*. Even though the isometric contraction is short and there is no movement, the muscles continue to develop greater tension. When the tension is sufficiently great (the start of the jump), muscle contraction immediately switches to the *concentric*, and the muscles shorten in their contraction. The concentric contraction — and how quickly and powerfully it takes place — is the key to the height achieved in the takeoff. The stronger the initial eccentric contraction and the faster the muscles contract in the concentric regime, the higher the jump.

Because all three muscle-contraction regimes are involved in the jump, all three must be improved on to maximize any increase in jump height. The more you load (tense) the muscles when getting ready for a jump, the higher you can go in the jump. In essence, the greater the tension and the faster the tension is created, the quicker you can execute the total jump and the higher you will go. This is why explosive training is so important. It develops the ability to execute a fast, high jump.

The muscles and tendons of the body are quite elastic. When they are stretched, they tend to contract more forcefully to return to their original shape. This is similar to a compressed spring or a stretched rubber band. For example, when you drop a basketball, the ball flattens somewhat upon striking the ground. Because the surface is elastic, it quickly returns to its original spherical form and

Frame 7

Frame 8

Frame 9

Frame 10

Frame 11

Frame 12

Figure 3-2 (cont'd)

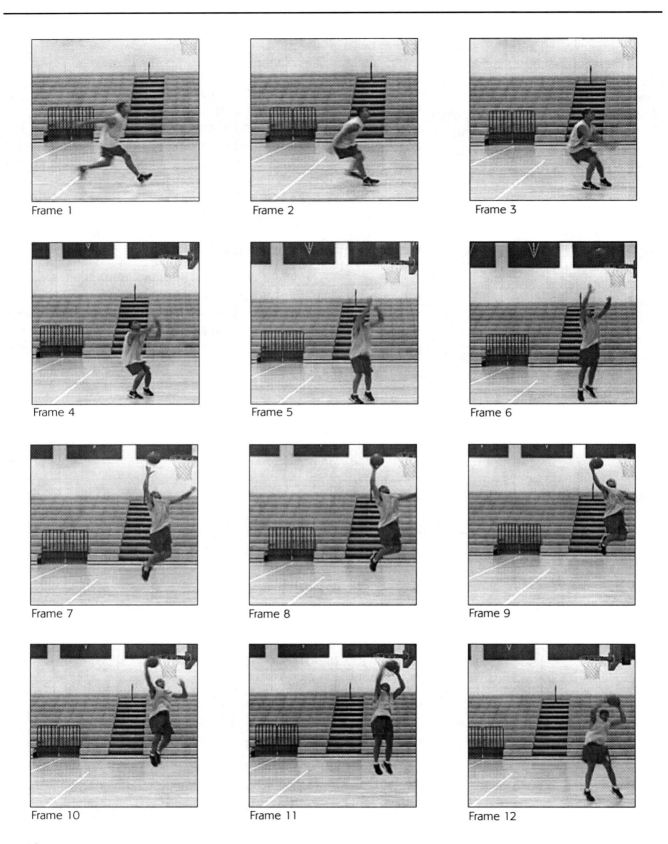

Frame 1 Frame 2 Frame 3

Frame 4 Frame 5 Frame 6

Frame 7 Frame 8 Frame 9

Frame 10 Frame 11 Frame 12

Figure 3-3

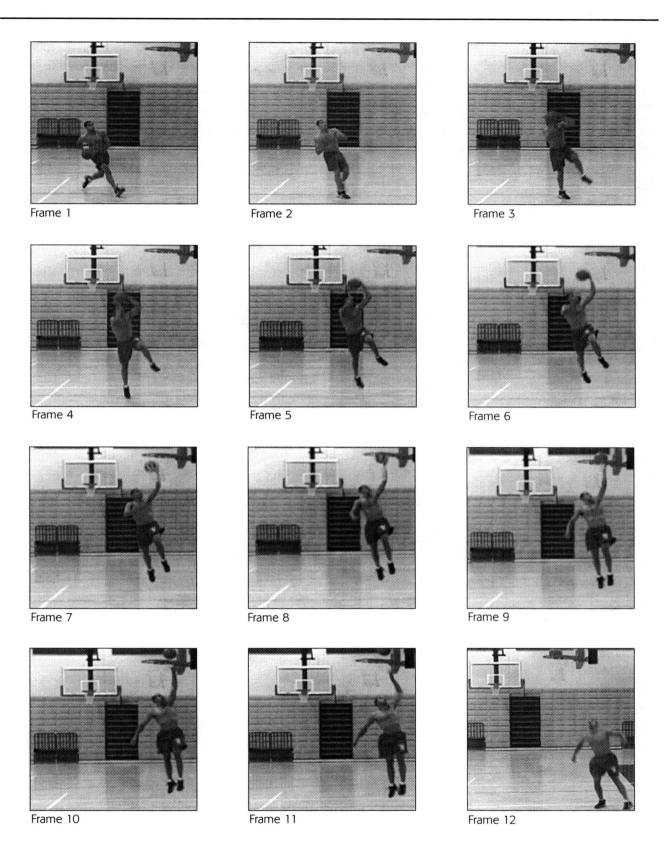

Frame 1

Frame 2

Frame 3

Frame 4

Frame 5

Frame 6

Frame 7

Frame 8

Frame 9

Frame 10

Frame 11

Frame 12

Figure 3-4

bounces, gaining most of its original speed. The height to which the ball bounces depends on the height from which it fell and its elasticity.

Using the elastic property of the muscles is one of the most important elements in improving jump height. The key is to create greater tension of the muscles and tendons in the preparation for a jump. Much of this force is developed during the landing or preparation (crouch) phase.

If you examine Figures 3-3, 3-4, and 3-5, you can see how muscle elasticity plays a big role in jumping. In Figure 3-5, the player jumps from a stationary position. Notice how he must go into a relatively deep squat (frames 3 through 5) to develop sufficient force and momentum to leap upward.

In Figures 3-3 and 3-4, the player has two different approaches, both of which generate forward momentum. Once the player lands, he does not go as deep in the squat to prepare the muscles

to leap upward as high as possible. In most cases, the leap is actually higher than can be attained in a stationary position.

Figure 3-6 is another example of elasticity. The player uses a faster approach. As soon as he hits and brings the other leg up, he does not go into as deep a squat as when stationary. He executes the jump faster (frames 1 through 4).

Strength and Speed

In preparing for a jump, the faster the downward movement or stopping action, the greater the tension (loading) of the muscles. Without the eccentric strength to quickly stop forward and downward movement, you cannot execute the most effective jump. Thus, you must determine the optimal approach speed for the strength you have. But the more strength you have and the faster your approach, the greater the tension that can be created in the jump preparation. When muscle and

Frame 1

Frame 2

Frame 3

Frame 4

Frame 5

Frame 6

Figure 3-5

tendon stretching is limited (through a short range of motion) but executed quickly and forcefully, it creates the greatest amount of usable tension (energy).

The eccentric and isometric muscle contractions that create the tension to stop forward and downward movement must be used quickly in the concentric contraction (together with any additional force developed in the muscles during the takeoff). This is known as *reactive force*. The jumper first directs all forces into the floor. Then the floor and the muscle and tendon energy push back to get his body airborne. The more developed or perfected your muscle and tendon elasticity, the quicker and better able your body and limbs will be to reform after being stretched. This results in efficient use of energy to jump more effectively.

Picture yourself standing on a table with a spring directly below and in front of you. You step off and land on the spring so that it is compressed and gains energy. It then returns to its original shape and (as a result) pushes you into the air. The muscles of the leg react in a similar manner. The muscles on both sides of the thigh act as springs, along with the Achilles tendon and the gastrocnemius and soleus muscles. When you go into a crouch the *springs* (muscles) are compressed (gain tension). When you take off, they return to the original position, and up you go. However, if you over-stretch the springs (the muscles and tendons), they will no longer have the ability to quickly return to their original shape.

Keep in mind that when the muscles are pre-tensed, they unleash a tremendous lifting force, which is much greater than any amount of strength developed by the muscles alone. Sheer strength is *not* the key to jump height! Most important is how much energy you can create in the preparation of the muscles and tendons through the eccentric and isometric contractions, and then how quickly you can switch the muscle contraction to the concentric to get you airborne with maximum height.

Frame 7

Frame 8

Frame 9

Frame 10

Frame 11

Figure 3-5 (cont'd)

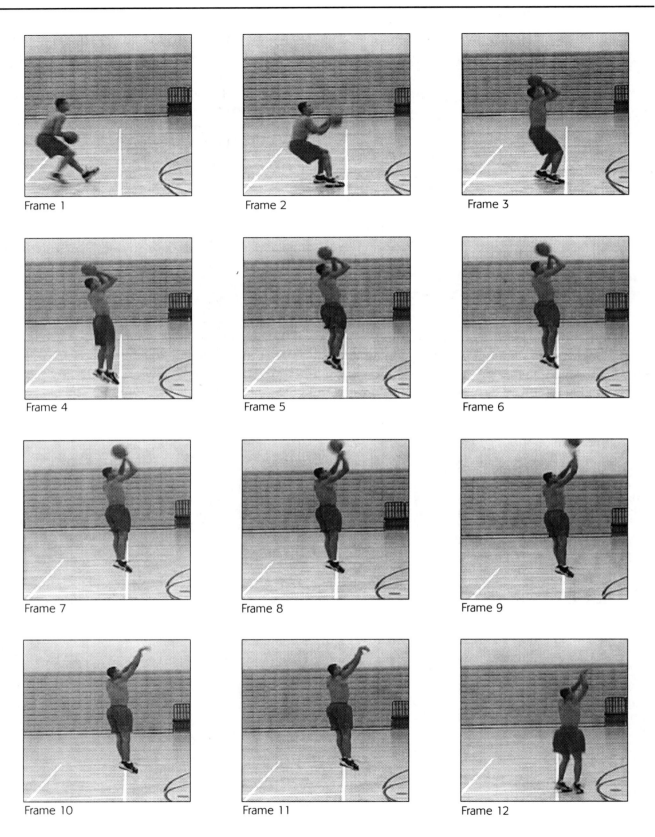

Frame 1   Frame 2   Frame 3

Frame 4   Frame 5   Frame 6

Frame 7   Frame 8   Frame 9

Frame 10   Frame 11   Frame 12

Figure 3-6

The execution of a pure act of strength is very slow. To execute squats with heavy weight (200 or more pounds), your movements must be slow. This explains why too much strength training, to the exclusion of other training, can be a negative to your jump performance. You need weight training to develop eccentric, concentric, and isometric strength, but once a sufficient amount is developed, you must convert pure strength to explosive strength (speed-strength). This is when explosive (power) exercises have their greatest value.

Executing the Jump

Let's look more closely at the precise actions involved in executing a jump. These occur in two phases: first, the preparation phase (the landing and crouch), and second, the takeoff phase. The purpose of the jump and what you do once airborne can vary greatly.

The Preparation Phase

In a jump from an approach (for example, a jump shot off the dribble), a player should strive for a strong eccentric contraction when stopping and getting ready. Combining this energy with the conversion of forward momentum results in vertical lift and height.

As you prepare for the jump, extend the forward leg and plant the heel on the floor well in front of the body. This stops lower-body forward momentum and gives the appearance of sitting back (Figure 3-1, frames 3 through 5; Figure 3-2, frames 1 and 2; Figure 3-6, frames 1 and 2). When the heel hits the ground, the force from the approach is driven into the legs, requiring the muscles to contract eccentrically to stop the forward movement and gain energy. The intensity of this contraction depends on the speed of the approach and stop.

As the planted leg bends, the other leg moves alongside it. The legs are bent at the ankles, knees and hips, and the trunk is basically erect. Both hands gather and hold the ball (Figure 3-1, frames 4 and 5; Figure 3-2, frame 2). From this position, you bring the ball up over the head. Leg extension begins and your weight moves upward. Once maximum tension in the muscles is developed, the actual jump begins. The muscles switch contractions (from eccentric to isometric to concentric). This produces a vertical takeoff (Figure 3-1, frames 5 through 7; Figure 3-2, frames 3 through 5; Figure 3-6, frames 3 through 5).

Without sufficient eccentric strength, the athlete cannot stop and convert forward momentum into vertical movement. Many athletes slow their approach or drift forward or laterally during the jump. A little forward movement is okay, but too much can affect a shooter's accuracy. In general, the greater your ability to stop forward momentum and convert all forces to the vertical, the higher the jump will be. This also leads to greater accuracy.

When you bring the other leg forward, it usually is placed to the side and slightly in front of the stopping leg. This gets you into a slightly angled position with the shooting arm and shoulder in front. In other words, the shoulders should be at a slight angle, so that your shooting arm is more in front and in line with your vision rather than having the shoulders square to the target.

The Landing

When preparing for touchdown, your feet should be directly under the hips to increase the leg muscles' efficiency. Landing should take place on the ball of the foot, followed immediately by the heel. At this time the ankle, knee, and hip joints undergo flexion. The key to a safe and effective touchdown is to land almost flat-footed so that the ball/heel contact occurs in quick succession. This allows the arch of the foot to absorb the initial shock and withstand most of the landing forces (Figure 3-7, frame 11; Figure 3-8, frame 10).

To ensure an effective and safe landing, tense the foot and leg muscles slightly while still in the air. Mentally and physically prepare for touchdown before making contact. This will keep you from going too low and dissipating the forces generated

Frame 1 Frame 2 Frame 3

Frame 4 Frame 5 Frame 6

Frame 7 Frame 8 Frame 9

Frame 10 Frame 11

Figure 3-7

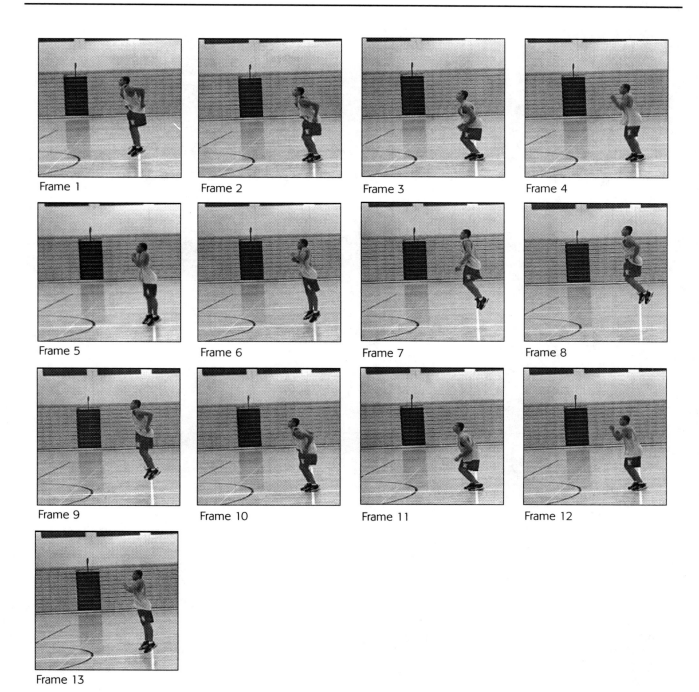

Frame 1

Frame 2

Frame 3

Frame 4

Frame 5

Frame 6

Frame 7

Frame 8

Frame 9

Frame 10

Frame 11

Frame 12

Frame 13

Figure 3-8

Frame 1

Frame 2

Frame 3

Frame 4

Frame 5

Frame 6

Frame 7

Frame 8

Frame 9

Frame 10

Frame 11

Frame 12

Figure 3-9

in case you have to jump again or go into action immediately.

The Takeoff

Once the muscles are tensed from the stopping action and down movement, you will be ready for a quick switch of muscle contractions to the concentric to produce an explosive takeoff. When there is time to execute the jump and an opponent is not close, most players take a shortened, relaxed jump. When close to an opponent or contesting a specific situation, the jump may be more explosive. This enables you to shoot over or out-rebound an opponent.

Other factors include whether you have the ball and whether the jump is made on the move or from a stationary position. The leg actions are basically the same. The arms play an important role, depending on the situation.

Takeoff Without the Ball

Most jumping occurs without the ball (rebounding, shot blocking, loose ball, jump ball). In these situations, the arms can assist in achieving maximum jump height   (Figures 3-3, 3-5 and 3-7 through 3-12). The arms play an important role in preparation of the leg muscles for the jump and in executing the takeoff.

For example, after you stop your forward momentum and the other leg is brought up alongside the stopping leg, the arms are brought backwards above hip height (Figure 3-3, frame 1; Figure 3-9, frame 3; Figure 3-11, frame 1). When going into the crouch, the arms drive downward and upward in an attempt to create even more force against the floor and get an even stronger eccentric contraction of the muscles involved. Greater muscle loading takes place when the arms make the curve at the bottom of the swing arc. When the arms go downward and then upward (in the bottom arc) the body weight is forced downward. This results in greater tension of the muscles involved, especially the all-important quadriceps.

On reaching the lowermost body position (which should not be too deep), the arms continue moving in an upward direction to unweight the body (Figure 3-3, frames 1 through 5; Figure 3-7, frames 3 through 7; Figure 3-9, frames 4 through 7; Figure 3-11, frames 1 through 4). The body becomes lighter because most of its weight is moving upward. The trunk begins to extend (hip-joint extension), the center of gravity is raised, and the body gains vertical momentum. The arms continue going upward with further lightening of the body. As the trunk continues to extend, it assumes a more vertical posture.

When the arms reach chest level, the knees extend and the body gains upward speed. When the trunk is extended directly over the hips, knee-joint extension should be concluding. All body parts are aligned vertically. The legs straighten and the ankle joints extend. The legs should be fully extended prior to the ankles achieving full extension (Figure 3-3, frames 3 through 6; Figure 3-7, frames 6 through 8; Figure 3-9, frames 4 through 7; Figure 3-10, frames 4 through 7; Figure 3-12, frames 2 through 6).

There is a definite sequence of actions in the jump. First is the arm movement coupled with trunk extension, followed by knee-joint and ankle-joint extension. While there is a slight overlap between each of these actions, they are sequenced to produce maximum summation of forces in the takeoff. At the exact moment of takeoff, the legs should be fully extended (completely straightened) and the toes should be pointed downward. The arms should be overhead (Figure 3-3, frame 6; Figure 3-7, frame 8; Figure 3-10, frame 7; Figure 3-11, frame 5; Figure 3-12, frame 6). The body rises until all forces generated in the takeoff are expended.

The faster the jump is executed, the higher you will go. This point cannot be over-emphasized. Speed and quickness of takeoff are the keys to attaining height. Look at some of the better jumpers at the professional and college levels, and you will see their jumps are executed quickly. They do not go into a deep squat or pause at the bottom of the squat before leaping. They make their approach, hit,

Frame 1 Frame 2 Frame 3
Frame 4 Frame 5 Frame 6
Frame 7 Frame 8 Frame 9
Frame 10 Frame 11 Frame 12

Figure 3-10

Frame 1   Frame 2   Frame 3

Frame 4   Frame 5   Frame 6

Frame 7   Frame 8   Frame 9

Frame 10   Frame 11   Frame 12

Figure 3-11

and leap. Always think in terms of speed of execution. Plant the foot, load the leg muscles, and take off.

In the takeoff, the quadriceps muscle is used to extend the knees. The gluteus maximus and hamstrings raise the trunk, and the gastrocnemius and soleus extend the ankle. These three joint actions must be executed quickly. In executing trunk extension (hip-joint extension), you have a little bit more time to raise the trunk to the vertical position.

For a quick takeoff, raising the trunk must be fast, but not necessarily as quick as the knee and ankle-joint actions. You can extend the trunk while loading the lower leg muscles.

Jump from a Standing Position

The stationary jump is basically the same as a jump with an approach. However, in a stationary position, you have no momentum to transfer or ability to load the muscles to the same extent in preparation for a

Frame 1   Frame 2   Frame 3

Frame 4   Frame 5   Frame 6

Frame 7   Frame 8   Frame 9

Figure 3-12

quick and powerful jump. From a standing position, you must bend the knees more to lower the body and load the muscles. There is more flexion in the ankle, knee, and hip joints as you go into a relatively deep crouch. This creates a longer range of motion, during which you can generate force for the takeoff.

As you lower the body, bring the arms up and to the rear in preparation for whipping the arms down and up during the takeoff. The quadriceps muscle plays a major role in this jump. When you go sufficiently deep, you also use the gluteus maximus and hamstrings. The key is to go down deeply and then use the muscles to generate the force needed to propel you upward. It is basically a down and upward movement, executed slower than in the approach run (Figure 3-5, frames 1 through 7; Figure 3-7, frames 1 through 7).

Jump with the Ball in the Hands

When holding a ball in the hands, the jump to shoot or pass is executed in exactly the same way, except that you do not have use of the arms to assist in achieving greater jump height. The key is to execute the jump as described, mainly the stopping action, by extending the leg out in front and allowing the body to move in over the legs before leaping when the ball is overhead (Figures 3-1, 3-2, and 3-6).

When stationary and holding a ball, it's necessary to go into a slightly deeper squat in order to get sufficient loading of the muscles for an effective takeoff. This is more important on longer, contested shots. On a short shot (such as free throw) the amount of bend can be less. As you go into the squat, the ball is brought up until it is overhead. At this time, you execute the jump (Figure 3-13, frames 1 through 5).

Frame 10

Frame 11

Frame 12

Frame 13

Frame 14

Frame 15

Figure 3-12 (cont'd)

Some players are still in the process of bringing the ball up before they complete the jump. This is fine as long as the ball is overhead at takeoff. Moving the ball upward is not as effective as having the ball overhead when you take off. When all the forces of your jump go into the ball, it gives you greater shooting distance after you reach maximum height. If you bring the ball up when you are airborne, you will decrease jump height.

The Lay-up

In the running lay-up, you have more approach speed than in any other jump and shot. You don't want to stop your forward momentum. Your main objective is to convert the forward momentum to vertical, ensuring a sufficiently high jump coupled with forward movement. To prepare for this change in direction, extend the forward leg as far out in front as possible in order to stop the lower body momentum and convert forward momentum into vertical momentum. If you do not convert the

horizontal forces to the vertical, you will find yourself flying through the air at a low height with little time to execute the lay-up.

Reducing lower-body horizontal momentum as much as possible (especially when running fast) demands exceptional eccentric strength, mainly in the quadriceps muscle. When planting the heel of the takeoff leg, leave the head and shoulders in place (to the rear) so the forward leg can effectively block the hips from continuing forward (Figure 3-14, frame 1; Figure 3-15, frame 1). The upper body continues forward and the stopping leg undergoes flexion (Figure 3-4, frames 1 and 2; Figure 3-14, frames 2 and 3; Figure 3-15, frames 2 and 3). The key is the eccentric strength of the muscles. This blocks the lower body's forward motion and prepares the muscles for a powerful concentric contraction.

On the vertical takeoff, the upper body continues moving forward. As it comes over the support (stopping) leg, the leg extends powerfully to

Frame 1   Frame 2   Frame 3

Frame 4   Frame 5   Frame 6

Figure 3-13

change horizontal movement to vertical. The extension in the hip, knee, and ankle joint must take place fairly rapidly because of the fast approach run. The faster and more powerful the leg extension, the greater the conversion to vertical height will be.

Because of the tremendous amount of forward momentum generated in a fast approach, even as you take off your body will continue to move forward to dissipate the momentum of the approach run. You execute the jump while your body is in motion. The key is to block your lower body momentum, but allow the upper body to continue moving forward. Execute the jump as your body comes over the takeoff leg. Then leap as high as possible to execute the lay-up as part of the forward movement. Greater leg strength results in faster approach runs and higher jumps (Figures 3-4, 3-14, and 3-15).

A Variation in Technique

The typical technique for the takeoff in the jump shot is to stop on one leg, bring the other leg up, and then take off from both feet. This technique has been used successfully for many years.

As the game has evolved, it has become necessary to execute a jump, especially for a jump shot, even faster than what can be done with the *step together* takeoff technique. The way to do this is to use a double-foot landing (jump stop) and takeoff. Not only can the jump be executed faster, you will be able to go higher than you can with the step-together approach. The reason for this is that you can more quickly and powerfully load the muscles. The takeoff takes place immediately after the initial landing, as opposed to waiting for the trailing leg to catch up with the leading leg.

Frame 7

Frame 8

Frame 9

Frame 10

Frame 11

Frame 12

Figure 3-13 (cont'd)

Frame 1

Frame 2

Frame 3

Frame 4

Frame 5

Frame 6

Frame 7

Frame 8

Frame 9

Frame 10

Frame 11

Figure 3-14

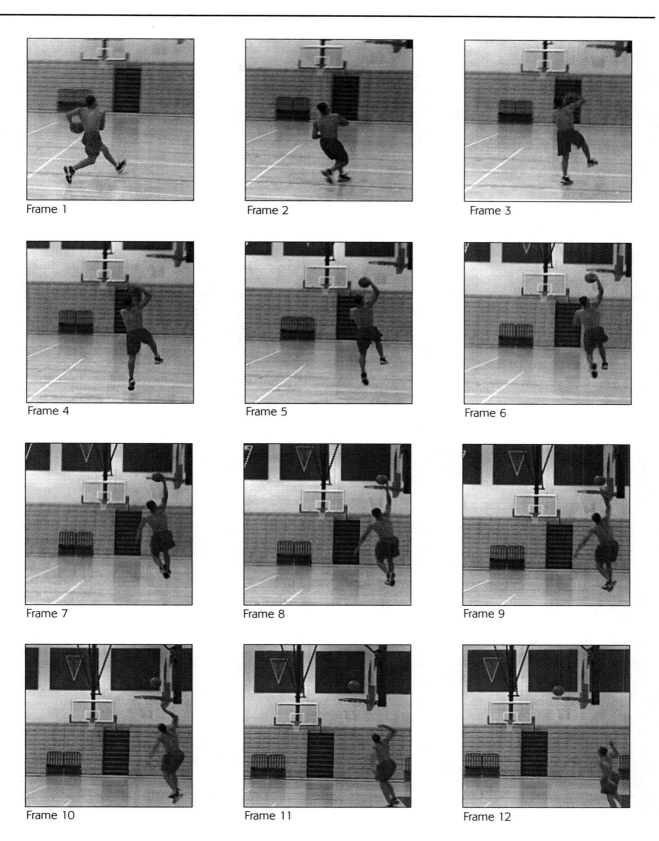

Frame 1

Frame 2

Frame 3

Frame 4

Frame 5

Frame 6

Frame 7

Frame 8

Frame 9

Frame 10

Frame 11

Frame 12

Figure 3-15

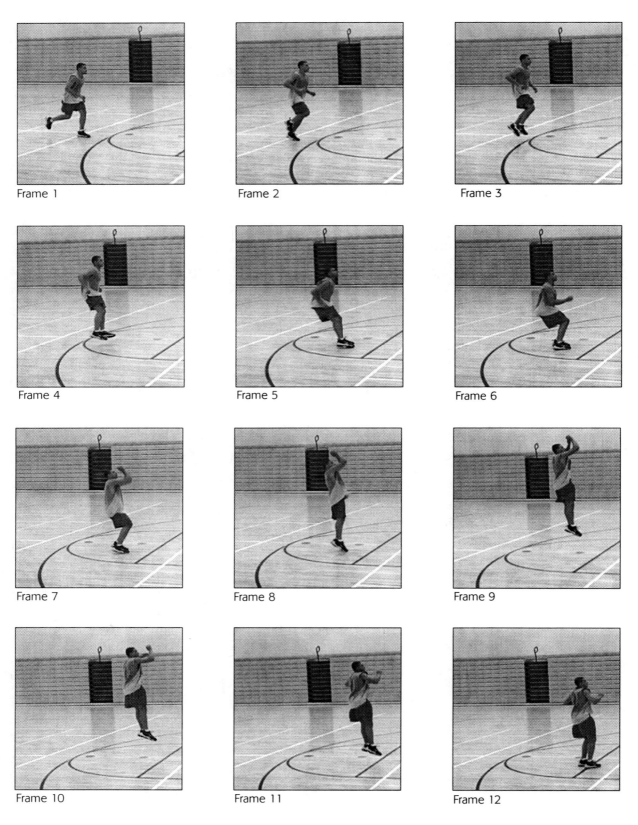

Frame 1

Frame 2

Frame 3

Frame 4

Frame 5

Frame 6

Frame 7

Frame 8

Frame 9

Frame 10

Frame 11

Frame 12

Figure 3-16

To execute the double-foot landing and takeoff, take off on one leg, leap through the air, and land on both feet. Then immediately leap up as high as possible (Figure 3-16). This takeoff is effective for jump shots, rebounds, tip-ins, and shot blocking. Quite often, you'll see a player use this action to create a jump shot off dribble penetration.

Notice that in Figure 3-16 the player does not sink low after both feet touch down on the floor (frames 5 and 6). If the player went into a deep squat, it would indicate lack of eccentric strength and detract from the effectiveness of the technique. By improving eccentric strength, the player can execute the jump even faster. By analyzing technique, it's possible to identify a player's physical weaknesses and design and prescribe exercises to improve performance.

CHAPTER 4

Specialized Exercises for Jumping

The following specialized exercises for jumping produce surprisingly fast results, and are based on the biomechanical and kinesiological analysis of effective jumping. They actually mimic the key actions in jumping. They duplicate the exact movements, range of motion, and types of muscular contraction involved. In the initial stages of training, these exercises may not duplicate the exact muscular contraction, as it is often necessary to prepare the muscles to do some of these exercises. Because of this, some of the exercises are done at different speeds, or with slight modifications before duplicating the exact conditions seen in explosive jumping for maximum height.

Biomechanical and kinesiological analyses of your abilities establish a baseline for improvement. From a biomechanical analysis of your jumping, it is possible to identify which joint actions are relatively weak, which are executed effectively, and which need modification. With this information, you can select exercises most suitable to your abilities and develop an effective workout program. Your training program should reflect your strengths and address your weaknesses.

If you participate in a general conditioning program, you may see some improvement in your jumping and overall play, especially if you were in poor shape when starting. But, if the strength and other exercises do not duplicate what you do in jumping, or if the exercises do not enhance your strong and weak points, you will not maximize improvement. However, general physical preparation can always serve as a strong base for doing specialized exercises.

To strengthen the muscles as needed in jumping, it is necessary to do a multitude of exercises, especially when first starting with general conditioning. You must involve all the major and minor muscles in many different exercises. Strengthening only the major muscles and ignoring some of the relatively minor muscles, especially of the foot and ankle, often leads to injury. You are only as strong as your weakest link.

To greatly improve your jumping, you must strengthen the muscles as they function in the key joint actions. Do at least one strength exercise for each major action involved. Also, use different speeds of execution to accustom the muscles to changes in jump height and quickness of execution.

You should do the following exercises to improve your technique and enhance your physical qualities. Since the key actions in jumping involve the agonist and the antagonistic muscles, you should do exercises for both sets of muscles in all three-muscle contraction regimes. In this way, you strengthen the muscles on both sides of the joint in all their actions, duplicating what occurs in the jump and reducing the chance of injury. The following exercise descriptions are divided into two groups: *Strength Exercises and Explosive Exercises.*

Strength Exercises

Use these nine exercises to develop the strength needed to maximize improvements in your jumping technique.

Heel Raises

This exercise strengthens the muscles involved in ankle-joint extension—the last joint action in the push-off.

Execution with rubber tubing: Stand on a stable board, two to four inches in height, on the balls of the feet so that the heels are free to move. Secure the middle of the rubber tubing around and under the balls of the feet, or under the platform or attachment board you are standing on. Attach the ends of the tubing to a non-slip belt (such as the one included in the Active Cords set mentioned in Chapter 1) fastened around the waist or to the handles, which can be held in the hands. Be sure there is adequate tension in the tubing when starting.

When ready, keep the legs straight and lower the heels until you feel a stretch in the Achilles' tendon. Then rise up as high as possible and hold for one to two seconds (Figures 4-1a and 4-1b). Lower the heels and repeat, going through a full range of motion on each repetition. If needed for balance, hold on to a stationary object.

Execution in the gym: Place the balls of your feet on the raised platform and your shoulders under the resistance lever pads of a calf-raise machine. Straighten the legs to assume an erect position. When ready, lower the heels until you feel a stretch of the Achilles tendon (Figure 4-1c). Rise up as high as possible and hold the up position for one to two seconds (Figure 4-1d). Lower the heels and repeat. Inhale and hold your breath on the rise. Exhale on the descent.

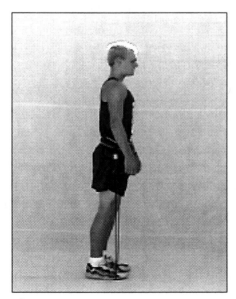

Figure 4-1a

Figure 4-1b

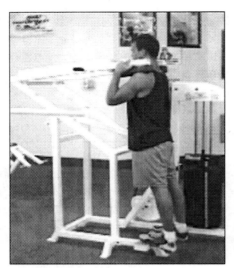

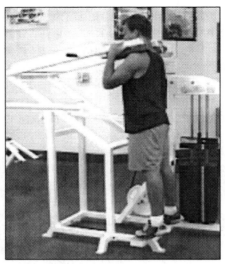

Figure 4-1c

Figure 4-1d

To develop assistive muscles and incorporate other foot actions, simply change foot positions. Point toes inward and rise up for greater strengthening of the tibialis anterior. Position toes outward to involve the peroneal muscles and the extensor digitorum longus located on the lateral sides of the shins. Always keep the feet hip-width apart during execution.

For development of greater balance, do this exercise on a raised platform, holding dumbbells in the hands or a barbell on the shoulders. Execution is the same but, because of the balance factor, you may use less weight to maintain stability. If you need support, do exercise with a dumbbell in one hand on a stairway. Hold the handrail for greater stability as you do the exercise on one leg.

Knee (Leg) Extensions

This exercise strengthens mainly the vastus lateralis and medialis muscles of the quadriceps femoris group. These muscles play a major role in keeping the patella in its groove, preventing some common knee problems.

Execution with rubber tubing: Assume a standing position with one end of rubber tubing attached to an ankle strap on the leg to be exercised, and the other end attached at knee or below-knee height. Stand with your back facing the non-movable attachment, but far enough away so there is some tension on the tubing. When ready, hold yourself erect, support yourself on a stationary object, or put your hand on an assistant for stability. Bring the knee up to about a 45-degree angle with the shin folded underneath, and then swing the shin out until the leg is straight. Return to the initial position and repeat. You will notice there is slight movement of the thigh upward as you completely extend the leg. This is an important safety factor and is more natural than immobilizing the thigh as in the typical leg extension exercise (Figures 4-2a and 4-2b).

Execution in the gym: The seated leg extension on a leg extension machine is a common exercise (Figures 4-2c and 4-2d). This can be effective, but it also has an element of danger because of the stationary thigh. During execution, great pressure is built up in the knee as the leg is extended, especially when there is great resistance. This can cause injury. It's recommended that you use the low cable pulley instead. It allows the knee to move so that you do the exercise in a more natural fashion.

Figure 4-2a

Figure 4-2b

Figure 4-2c

Figure 4-2d

Figure 4-2e

Figure 4-2f

Execution on a low cable is basically the same as with rubber tubing. Stand facing away from the cable pulley to which the leg is attached with the thigh raised approximately 45 degrees. Straighten the leg fully, return to the initial position, and repeat (Figures 4-2e and 4-2f). If you do this exercise on a leg extension machine, go through half the range of motion. Begin with the knee at a 45-degree angle, and then extend the leg until it is straight. Return to the 45- degree angle and repeat. To target the vastus lateralis and medialis, fully extend the leg. Do not use extremely heavy resistance. Instead, do more repetitions. This reduces the chance of injury.

Knee (Leg) Curls

This exercise strengthens hamstring muscles and the tendons that cross the knee to create a more stable knee joint. Hamstring muscle development is important in balancing the strength of the quadriceps on the front of the thigh. The quadriceps should always be stronger. Although the exact ratio may vary, it appears to be close to a 3:1 or 4:1 ratio. The stronger the hamstrings, the more the quadriceps may be strengthened.

Execution with rubber tubing: Assume a standing position with one leg raised 45 to 60 degrees to the horizontal and one end of the tubing attached to the ankle strap. Secure the free end of the cord about chest or hip high. When ready, hold the thigh in place and bend the knee to bring the shin under the thigh. Return to the initial position and repeat (Figure 4-3a and 4-3b).

Execution in the gym: This exercise usually is done lying facedown on a knee curl machine. Most popular is the facedown position on an angled bench. The knees should be free of support. The backs of the lower shins should rest against the underside of the resistance rollers. When ready, raise your feet by bending the knees until the shins are slightly past the vertical position. Return under control to the initial position and repeat (Figures 4-3c and 4-3d).

You can also do the knee curl exercise using a relatively low or high cable pulley machine. To execute, stand facing the pulley with the leg extended and raised in front approximately 45 degrees. When ready, keep the thigh in place and bend the knee joint to bring the shin under the thigh. Return the shin to the straight-leg position and

Figure 4-3a

Figure 4-3b

Figure 4-3c

Figure 4-3d

repeat. You will notice that the thigh acts a safety valve. There can be slight movement of the thigh together with the knee, simulating what takes place in jumping and running (Figures 4-3e and 4-3f).

The Squat

The squat is the main exercise to improve jumping. It duplicates closely the exact motions involved in jumping. It strengthens the quadriceps femoris muscle group, the hamstrings and the gluteus maximus, especially if you go sufficiently deep. The squat is a good exercise to prevent knee problems.

Execution with rubber tubing: Place the middle of the rubber tubing under both feet and hold the handles attached to the waist belt or to the ends in

the hands held hip or shoulder high. When in a standing position, there should be strong tension on the cords. Stand with your feet approximately hip-width apart and your toes pointed straight ahead or turned out slightly (Figure 4-4a).

Inhale and hold your breath. Flex your knees and slowly lower your body into the squat position, keeping your heels in contact with the floor and the lower back in its normal curvature. The knees should move forward slightly. The buttocks should move slightly to the rear and then straight down. The trunk should incline forward up to 45 degrees from the vertical in the down position. Be sure to maintain a slight arch in the lower back at all times (Figure 4-4b).

Figure 4-3e

Figure 4-3f

Figure 4-4a

Figure 4-4b

After reaching the bottom position, reverse directions by forcefully extending the legs and rise up. When you pass the most difficult portion of the up phase, exhale and complete the exhalation when in a full standing position. Keep your eyes focused directly in front. The bottom position is determined by your ability to hold the arch in the lower back. If your spine begins to round in the down position you should stop your descent immediately. The point at which the back rounding occurs determines how far you lower the body.

Execution in the gym: Stand with your feet approximately shoulder-width apart and toes

pointed straight ahead or turned out slightly. Hold dumbbells in the hands or a barbell behind the neck across the shoulders and resting on the upper trapezius muscle. Execute the same as with rubber tubing (Figures 4-4c through 4-4e). Repeat at a moderate rate of speed. For variety, lower the body at a moderate rate of speed and rise up quickly.

Variant – Delay squat with tubing or barbell: The delay squat is an effective exercise for increasing eccentric and isometric strength. It also helps develop the explosive contraction at the peak of maximum tension in the muscle. To execute, do the squat exercise as indicated above except for the

Figure 4-4c

Figure 4-4d

Figure 4-4e

following changes. As you begin, lower the body very slowly four to six inches in four seconds. After the initial count of four, hold the position for another count of four. Begin lowering the body very slowly for another count of four, followed by a hold for a count of four. Repeat for a third time. After holding the down position, come up for as quickly as possible, jumping as forcefully as you can. Because of the resistance, you will be unable to leave the floor, but you will develop the explosiveness of the muscle at the maximum tension.

The Good Morning (Arched Back Bend-Over)

This exercise duplicates a portion of the raising of the trunk in the jump take-off. In addition, it increases the stabilization strength of the lower back in its normal curvature, and stretches and strengthens the hamstring muscles and their upper tendons. It is executed most effectively with dumbbells in the hands or a barbell on the shoulders.

Execution: Stand erect with a barbell on the shoulders or holding dumbbells in the hands shoulder high. Your feet should be approximately hip- to shoulder-width apart. The legs should be straight or slightly bent, and the lumbar spine should be in its normal alignment, with a slight arch at all times.

When ready, inhale slightly more than usual and hold your breath as you bend forward from the hip joints. Push your hips backward as your trunk inclines forward and down to the horizontal position (or as far as your flexibility will allow). After reaching the lowermost position, reverse directions and rise up to the starting position. Exhale as you approach the upright position (Figures 4-5a and 4-5b, for execution with dumbbells; Figure 4-5c, for execution with a barbell on the shoulders). More weight places greater stress on the lower back muscles. If holding dumbbells shoulder-high is too difficult, hold them on extended arms about hip high.

Glute-Ham-Gastroc Raises

This exercise is done to strengthen the hamstring muscles and their tendons at the hip and knee joints. The glute-ham-gastroc raise is especially valuable in the prevention and rehabilitation of hamstring injuries. It has been reported that basketball players (especially guards who sprint and cut throughout the game) have never had a hamstring injury when this exercise is executed on a regular basis. It develops hamstring muscles through

Figure 4-5a

Figure 4-5b

Figure 4-5c

the same range of motion and action as used in jumping and running.

Execution: Do this exercise on the Yessis Back Machine (pictured in Figure 4-6), also known as the Glute-Ham Machine (the name first given to this machine by the author, who invented this machine and introduced this exercise in the U.S.). Assume a facedown position so that support is on the upper thighs when the feet are placed between the rear rollers for support. When your legs are in place, lower your trunk over and down the front side of the seat and hold the back in its normal curvature. Your upper body and pelvic girdle should form a straight line from the hip joint to the head (Figure 4-6a).

Inhale slightly (but more than usual) and hold your breath as your raise your trunk with the axis in the hips. Your back should remain rigid in its slightly arched position. Raise your trunk until the body forms a straight line from your head to your feet (Figure 4-6b). With the hip-joint extensor muscles under contraction, bend your knees. Raise your straight body to approximately a 30-degree angle above the horizontal (Figure 4-6c).

After reaching the top position, exhale and relax slightly, but keep the lower back in its slightly arched position. Lower your body by straightening the legs and then flex at the hips to return to the original position. Execute the exercise at a moderate rate of speed.

Back Raises

Back raises strengthen the lower back, which must be strong and stable during the jumping action and

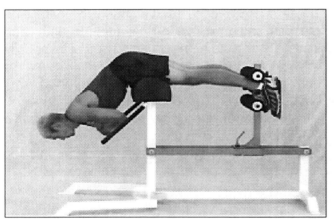

Figure 4-6a

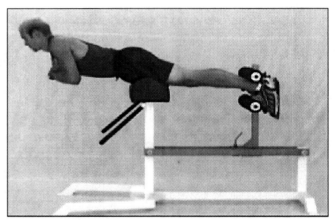

Figure 4-6b

Figure 4-6c

other actions. In this way, the forces from the legs may be transferred up through the midsection to the upper body and arms. The back raise is also the best exercise for the prevention of lower back problems.

Execution: Back raises are conveniently and safely done on the Yessis Back Machine (formerly the Glute-Ham Machine). If you do not have this machine available to you, use a high sturdy table with an assistant holding down your legs. Position yourself face-down over the curved seat of the Yessis Back Machine so that when your feet are placed between the rear pads, your entire pelvic girdle rests on the seat. Lower your upper body over the seat and relax the spinal muscles. In this position, your spine will naturally assume a rounded position, at approximately a 60-degree angle below the horizontal (Figure 4-7a). Your legs should be fully extended and straight at all times.

From the down position, inhale slightly more than usual and hold your breath as you extend (straighten) your spine to raise the upper body until it is higher than your legs (Figure 4-7b). Hold the uppermost position for one to two seconds and then exhale and return to the original position under control. When you reach the lowermost position, relax your muscles and repeat.

Reverse-Back Raises

If you are uncomfortable when your trunk is in an upside-down position (as in back raises) do the reverse-back raise. Position yourself in the opposite manner on the Yessis Back Machine or a high sturdy table. The lower abdomen should be directly atop the rounded seat, and the legs should hang down at approximately a 60-degree angle. Your hands should hold the back plate or rollers to stabilize the upper body (Figure 4-8a). When ready, inhale and raise the legs until they are above the level of the trunk (Figure 4-8b). Exhale as you lower the legs and repeat.

For greater resistance, use ankle weights (as in photos) or rubber tubing. To execute with rubber tubing, place the attachment board under the front supports of the machine to secure it, and attach both ends of the rubber tubing to the hook directly under the legs. Wrap the middle of the cord around both legs. There should be slight tension on the tubing when you are in the down position. When ready, inhale and hold your breath as you raise the leg(s) until they are in line with or slightly higher than the level of your back. Exhale and return to the initial position. Relax for a moment and repeat. Keep the legs straight during execution.

Front-Arm Raises

Front-arm raises increase the strength of the shoulder muscles involved in whipping the arms down and up in preparation for the takeoff.

Execution: Assume a face-up position on an incline bench, inclined at 45 to 60 degrees from the

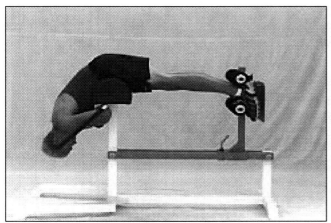

Figure 4-7a

Figure 4-7b

vertical, or on a flat bench. Hold a relatively light dumbbell in each hand, and keep the elbows slightly flexed. Do not hyperextend the arms. When ready, inhale and hold your breath as you hold the relatively straight-arm position, and raise the arms until they are vertical, directly above the head. Lower the arms and exhale as you return to the initial position under control. Repeat as needed (Figures 4-9a and 4-9b).

Explosive Exercises

Use these 12 exercises to develop the explosive power needed to maximize improvements in your jumping technique. Most of these exercises are plyometric jumps.

Squat Jumps

Squat jumps have two main purposes. They develop the ability to switch the eccentric and isometric contractions to the concentric, ensuring a quicker takeoff, especially when jumping repeatedly as in rebounding. They also develop eccentric strength through a greater range of motion. This helps stop the down action of the body after landing from a jump.

Execution: Assume a standing position with the feet directly under the hips. When ready, bend the knees and descend into a half-squat, then explode upward as high as possible. Be sure the ankles are fully extended and the legs are straight on takeoff. Prepare for the landing as you are coming down. Immediately after touchdown, cushion some of the shock and allow the body to sink down to the bottom position. Immediately jump up again as high as possible. Be sure to inhale and hold your breath during the landing and takeoff and exhale quickly when airborne. Quickly inhale as you prepare to land and repeat (Figure 4-10, frames 1 through 9). To increase the explosive strength component, do the exercise holding dumbbells (10 to 20 pounds).

Split Squat Jumps

This exercise develops the strength needed for an off-balance or split-leg landing. Ideally, you should land with both feet directly under the hips. Many times this is impossible, depending upon what happens when you are airborne. Prepare yourself for landings on one foot or with the feet spread, and you'll reduce the likelihood of injury.

Execution: Assume a standing position with the feet under the hips. If you are very strong, hold a 10 to 20 pound dumbbell in each hand. When ready, go into a slight crouch and leap up as high as possible. Once you are airborne, split the legs with one leg going forward and the other backward. Land in the stride position. Immediately after landing, jump back up and scissor the legs again. Repeat in an alternating manner. The key is to leap up as high as possible with full ankle-joint extension and straightening of the legs (Figure 4-11, frames 1 through 8). When using

Figure 4-8a

Figure 4-8b

Figure 4-9a

Figure 4-9b

weights, jump height decreases greatly. Do both variants for maximum benefit.

Jump Out of a Squat

This exercise develops reaction time and improves jumping – useful attributes in a jump-ball situation. It also improves quickness when taking the first step in a cutting or reaching action.

Execution: Assume a half squat or slight crouch position. The legs should have approximately a 145-degree angle in the knee joints, and the trunk should be inclined forward slightly. Hold the position for two to five seconds, then leap up as forcefully as possible. After landing, go into the same position and hold, ready to repeat (Figure 4-12). Do this exercise with weights once you've developed strength and explosiveness.

When working on reaction time, have someone give you a signal to start. The signal should be auditory or visual and vary in intensity. For example, the command could be quiet, loud, or anywhere in between. When using visual signals, have slight movement of the hand indicate a go, or use full movement of the hand or other body part to signal the start. When working on quickness in the first step, instead of leaping directly upward, leap in the intended direction of movement.

For example, on the hand signal forward take a quick first step. If the signal is to the rear, take a quick first step to the rear. The same applies moving left and right. Be ready to react to movement in any direction. Don't anticipate where the movement is going to go. In this way, you will develop the reactive ability needed to keep up with an opponent who tries to evade you with quick actions. You'll also learn to react to various signals.

Double-Leg Jumps in Place

This exercise develops the kind of explosive power needed to be effective beneath and around the basket.

Execution: Assume a standing position with the feet directly under the hips. When ready, bend the legs slightly, swing the arms down and around, and leap up as high as possible with full extension of the legs. Make sure the legs are straight and toes are pointed. On touchdown, land close to the arch of the foot, (on the ball and then the heel of the foot almost simultaneously). Cushion yourself slightly, then jump up fast. Execute the landing and takeoff as quickly as possible. It must be explosive! Prepare yourself mentally and physically for each landing and takeoff (Figure 4-13).

Double-Leg Jumps With a 180-Degree Turn

These jumps develop explosive jumping ability and greater coordination when airborne. Execute the double-leg jump as in Figure 4-13. When you are

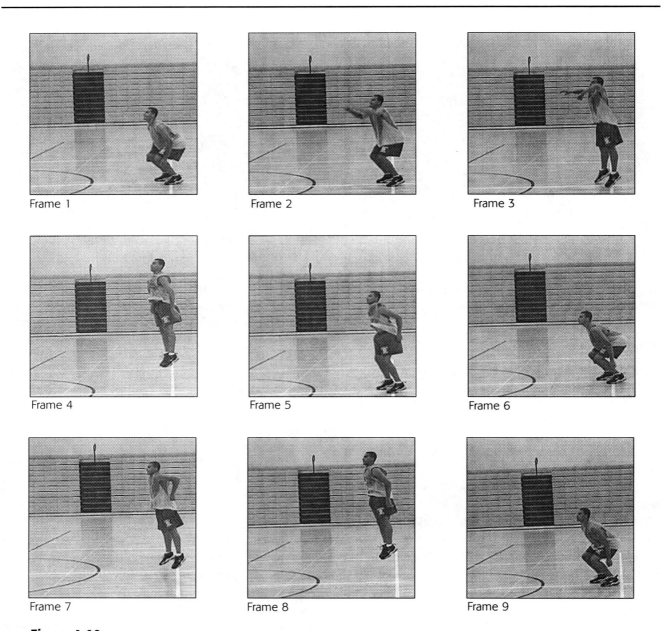

Frame 1   Frame 2   Frame 3

Frame 4   Frame 5   Frame 6

Frame 7   Frame 8   Frame 9

Figure 4-10

airborne, turn the body a full 180 degrees, so that when you land you are facing in the opposite direction. Immediately upon touchdown, leap up again as quickly as possible and turn a full 180 degrees back to the original facing position. Alternate the turns to the right and left for a full 180 degrees. To increase the difficulty, incorporate some traveling on each jump. Travel no more than about 12 inches on each jump and be sure you move in a straight line (Figure 4-14, frames 1 through 12).

When first starting this exercise, you may have difficulty traveling in a straight line.

Double-Leg Jumps with a 90-Degree Turn

If you find the 180-degree turn too difficult, begin with 90-degree turns and build up to 180 degrees (Figure 4-15). As you execute these jumps, be sure that you travel in a straight line. Traveling zigzag indicates that you are off-balance when executing the turn.

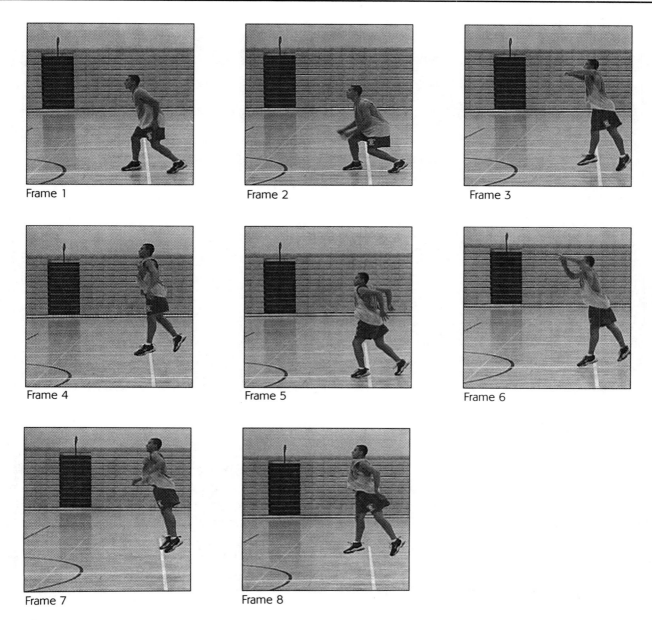

Frame 1 Frame 2 Frame 3

Frame 4 Frame 5 Frame 6

Frame 7 Frame 8

Figure 4-11

Single-Leg Jumps in Place

This exercise improves your ability to land and take off on one leg. Landing on one leg after a jump is not recommended as the forces are twice those of landing on both legs and can be up to 15 or more times your body weight. These are extremely high forces that can easily cause injury if your muscles are not sufficiently strong. This exercise helps prevent injury in those cases when you must land on one leg. It also improves jumping, as for example on the lay-up when you take off on one leg. The key is to leap as high as possible in a vertical direction and to execute the landing and takeoff as quickly as possible.

Execution: Stand on one leg in a well-balanced position. When you are ready, swing your arms down and around and then up. As the arms come up, drive the swing leg knee upward. At the same time, fully straighten the support leg and strongly extend the ankle joint to leap as high as possible.

Frame 1　　Frame 2　　Frame 3

Frame 4　　Frame 5　　Frame 6

Figure 4-12

Prepare for the landing mentally and physically. When you make ground contact, cushion and execute another quick jump upward (Figure 4-16, frames 1 through 7).

Ankle Jumps

Ankle jumps ensure that you use the full range of ankle-joint extension in jumping. Not using the ankle and relying mainly on the knee-joint extension is perhaps the biggest fault that has been found when analyzing basketball players' jumps. This exercise accentuates ankle action so you can incorporate it in the full jump. Ankle jumps are also beneficial in improving running and cutting speed. Prior to doing this exercise, do the explosive-heel raise exercise described in Chapter 8.

Execution: Assume a standing position with the feet directly under the hips. Keep the legs slightly bent, and concentrate on jumping solely with ankle-joint extension. Eliminate knee-joint actions as much

as possible. The range of motion in the knee joint should be no more than 10 to 15 degrees, while the ankle joint goes through the full range of motion (60 to 80 degrees). The toes should be pointed downward on every jump and the legs should be straight on takeoff (Figure 4-17, frames 1-6 and frames 7-8 for side view).

Step-Up Jumps

This exercise develops explosive power from a one-legged jump and greater coordination between left- and right-leg actions.

Execution: Assume a standing position in front of a bench, bleachers, or a platform approximately knee high. Place one foot on the seat and keep the other leg on the floor. The thigh of the leg on the bench should be level so that there is approximately a 90-degree angle in the knee-joint. When ready, push off with the leg on the bench to raise your body. As your leg straightens, leap as high as

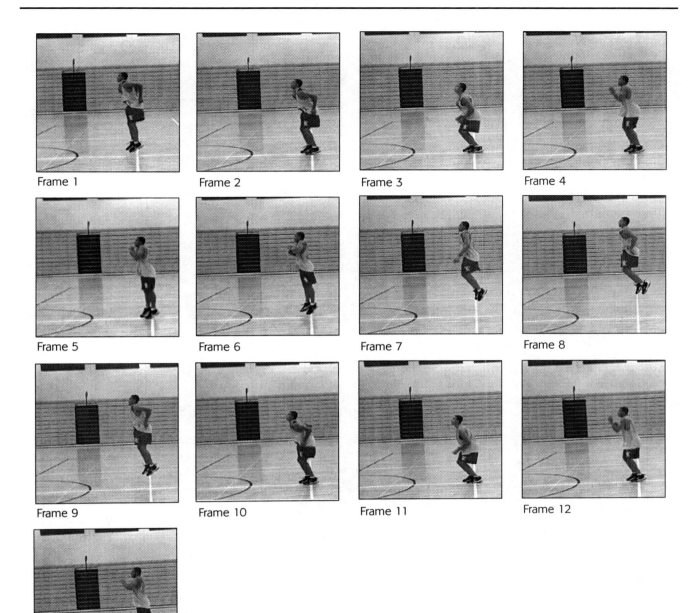

Frame 1

Frame 2

Frame 3

Frame 4

Frame 5

Frame 6

Frame 7

Frame 8

Frame 9

Frame 10

Frame 11

Frame 12

Frame 13

Figure 4-13

Frame 1

Frame 2

Frame 3

Frame 4

Frame 5

Frame 6

Frame 7

Frame 8

Frame 9

Frame 10

Frame 11

Frame 12

Figure 4-14

possible. Land on the bench with the opposite foot and the jump leg on the floor. Leap up again in the same fashion. Alternate legs on every jump. The key here is to leap as high as possible on each jump with full leg- and ankle-joint extension (Figure 4-18, frames 1-6).

Depth Jumps

Depth jumps improve jump height, or more specifically, explosive power in the legs. They also improve quickness, running speed, and cutting actions.

Execution: Stand on a raised platform, on the first row of the bleachers, or some other stationary object that is 12 to 24 inches high. When ready, step out with one leg and then drop straight down fairly close to the platform (Figure 4-19). The key is to drop down in a straight line so there are no forward forces to contend with. Prepare yourself physically and mentally for the landing. Land almost flat-footed, cushion yourself somewhat, and immediately jump up as high as possible as quickly as possible. Contact and takeoff should take no longer than .15 seconds.

Jump straight up after making contact with the ground. Do not execute any other actions after the jump. The key is to concentrate on the landing and takeoff, not on what you will be doing afterwards.

Depth jumps are a form of *shock training*. As you drop down from a height, your body is accelerating. At the moment of contact with the ground, the muscles undergo a very powerful contraction to keep you from sinking too low and to gain the energy needed to leap as high as possible. There is a shock to the body upon landing. The key is how quickly you execute the landing and takeoff. If you find yourself going very deep, you are stepping off from too great a height, or you do not have sufficient eccentric strength to slow you down and stop you before leaping upward. In such cases, do additional strength training for eccentric and isometric strength, or lower the height from which you step off.

The height of the jump is important. Very tall players should not use very high heights. If you are strong and approximately six-feet tall, you can step off a platform that is approximately 30 inches in height. Do not go any higher. The forces experienced from greater heights create a tendency to sink too low and force you to execute the takeoff slower than what is called for. Also, because of the high-impact forces, very tall players should step off platforms no higher than 24 inches. Depth jumps are valuable in your arsenal of exercises, but they should be used intelligently.

Medicine-Ball Throw Backward

This exercise improves your jumping ability by emphasizing an explosive contraction of the leg muscles and ensures that you get full extension of the body. When you have full extension, you see a slightly arched body when airborne. The key is to leap as high as possible as you fully extend the body to throw the ball backwards. Mastery of this exercise can help greatly in jumping and getting rebounds and tip-ins (see Figure 3-11, frame 6, in Chapter 3).

Execution: Stand holding a medicine ball in two arms below the waist. When you ready, bend the knees slightly, incline the trunk, and go into a slight crouch. Then raise the trunk, leap off the floor, keep the arms straight, and throw the ball over your head as high and as far back as possible. When first starting this exercise get the feel of throwing the ball backward with only the arms, then gradually incorporate use of the legs. Begin with easy throws and gradually build up to full power (Figure 4-20).

Medicine-Ball Throw Forward

This exercise also has a dual purpose. It improves jumping ability and helps ensure that you get full extension of the body while traveling upward and forward (as opposed to upward and slightly backward as in Figure 4-20).

Execution: Stand holding a medicine ball in two hands below the waist. When ready, bend the knees slightly, incline the trunk, and go into a slight crouch. Then raise the trunk, straighten the legs, and leap off the floor. As you take off, keep the arms straight and throw the ball up and forward as high and as far

Frame 1

Frame 2

Frame 3

Frame 4

Frame 5

Frame 6

Frame 7

Frame 8

Frame 9

Frame 10

Frame 11

Frame 12

Figure 4-15

forward as possible. When starting this exercise, get the feel of throwing the ball upward and forward with only the arms. Gradually incorporate the legs. Begin with easy throws and slowly build up to full power (Figure 4-21, frames 1 through 4).

General Recommendations for Jump Training

- When first starting speed-strength (explosive) training, keep the intensity low. To increase intensity, gradually increase the height of the jumps.

- Begin with double-leg jumps. Move on to single-leg jumps when ready.

- Gradually increase the volume (repetitions) of jumping in the initial stages of training. As you move into the specialized period of training, increase the intensity (height) of jumping and decrease the volume. (This is analogous to what you do in the progression of changes in weight training.)

- When you first start jump training, jump on surfaces that are neither too hard nor too soft and are somewhat resilient. For example, use gymnastic and wrestling mats, gym floors, a grassy field, etc. Never do jump training on concrete.

- For general strengthening of the foot and ankle joint to help prevent injury, do some barefoot running and easy jumping.

- Always execute lead-up or preparatory jumps before doing true full-intensity plyometric jumps.

- Always land on both feet except when doing single-leg jumps. When you land on one foot, you have twice the amount of force in comparison to landing on both feet.

Frame 1

Frame 2

Frame 3

Frame 4

Frame 5

Frame 6

Frame 7

Figure 4-16

Frame 1 Frame 2 Frame 3 Frame 4

Frame 5 Frame 6 Frame 7 Frame 8

Figure 4-17

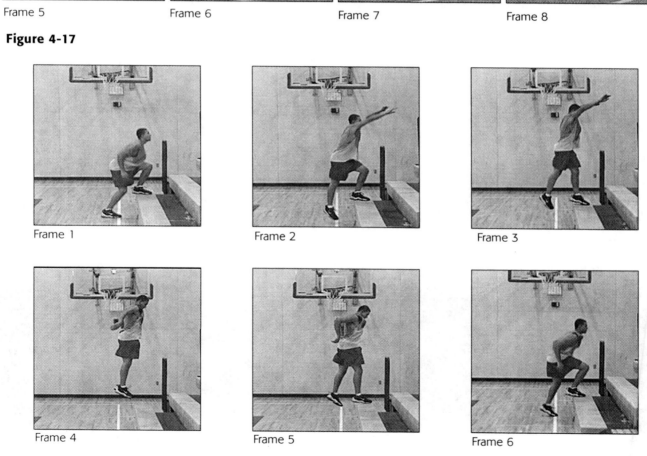

Frame 1 Frame 2 Frame 3

Frame 4 Frame 5 Frame 6

Figure 4-18

Frame 1　　　　　Frame 2　　　　　Frame 3　　　　　Frame 4

Frame 5　　　　　Frame 6　　　　　Frame 7

Figure 4-19

Frame 1　　　　　Frame 2

Frame 3　　　　　Frame 4

Figure 4-20

- In the early stages of training, do only two to three explosive exercises for one set of no more than 10 repetitions.

- As you develop the ability to do high-intensity jump exercises effectively, you can add more exercises and sets to the program. Do not increase number of repetitions in one set.

- In general, do no more than 6 to 10 consecutive explosive-jump exercises, especially when doing two to three sets each.

- Be sure that you begin jump exercises after an adequate warm-up and after you have completed the active stretches. All jumps should precede lower-body and mid-section strength training.

Frame 1

Frame 2

Frame 3

Frame 4

Figure 4-21

CHAPTER 5

Improving Shooting Range and Accuracy

Surprisingly, few basketball players and coaches fully understand the unique relationship between shooting accuracy and power. To maximize range and accuracy – let's call it *effective* range – and to score baskets over and around defenders, you must build strength and master technique. This is not nearly as easy as it sounds, and here's why.

To increase range, you must increase the number of movements of the body and body parts and have a greater range of motion (ROM) in each of the actions. To improve accuracy, you must precisely limit the ROM of each action, as well as the number of body parts involved. It's a delicate balancing act and extremely difficult to achieve. This is why few players, including professionals, achieve great success as shooters.

Shooting for maximum distance and accuracy requires a tremendous amount of practice *and* greater levels of strength to withstand the forces involved in producing maximum power. Without a specific set of physical strengths, injury is likely to occur. As you develop greater strength, you must also develop the muscular feel needed to develop, maintain, and improve accuracy. But even as hard as this sounds, it is doable.

A simple but effective way to improve range is to involve the legs in the shooting action. This is why the *jump* portion of the jump shot is so important. As you prepare to shoot, you go into a slight crouch, then extend the legs as you bring the arms up to execute the shot at the top of your jump (height). In this way, some force from the legs is transferred through the body into the ball to give you greater range. For this to occur, however, you need a strong midsection and breath control to make the trunk rigid. Many players also incorporate use of the legs to develop a shooting rhythm and give the ball some momentum before executing the shot with the arms. You see this technique in many players' foul shots.

Players with insufficient strength often incorporate a strong jump, leaving the floor at an angle toward the basket. As a result, after the ball is released, they fly through the air and land several feet in front of their takeoff point. Youngsters often use this method to increase their range.

To release a jump shot at maximum height, you must jump in a vertical direction with little or no horizontal drift. This implies that the shot is executed with the shooting arm only. Additional momentum

Frame 1

Frame 2

Frame 3

Frame 4

Frame 5

Frame 6

Frame 7

Frame 8

Frame 9

Frame 10

Frame 11

Frame 12

Figure 5-1

Frame 1

Frame 2

Frame 3

Frame 4

Frame 5

Frame 6

Frame 7

Frame 8

Frame 9

Figure 5-2

may be imparted to the ball from the jump. In this case, the legs do not add as much force (and range) to the ball distance (except if the ball is released on the rise). The jump height, however, does shorten the distance that the ball must travel and makes the trajectory of the ball more favorable.

Strength plays a central role in the ability to shoot accurately and at long range. You must have adequate strength of the shoulder, arm, and wrist muscles (the shooting mechanism), combined with adequate strength of the leg muscles to propel you upward. This is why the best shooters in younger age groups are often simply the strongest players. The shooting pattern you develop when you are young depends to a great extent on the strength you possess at that time.

A stronger player uses more powerful arm, shoulder, and wrist actions, together with a higher

Frame 1　　　Frame 2　　　Frame 3

Frame 4　　　Frame 5　　　Frame 6

Frame 7　　　Frame 8　　　Frame 9

Frame 10　　　Frame 11　　　Frame 12

Figure 5-3

jump. The weaker (or younger) player executes *an arm* shot with a simultaneous push of the legs. Both the arms and legs are needed to generate sufficient force to reach the basket. See Figure 5-1 for an example of this push pattern used by weaker players and youngsters to achieve maximum distance. The legs generate most of the weaker shooter's range, since they are stronger than the arms. In this push pattern, the legs push the body upward as the arms push the ball to the basket.

Overlapping arm and leg actions generate sufficient power, but reduce accuracy. By increasing strength levels in specific areas, accuracy can be improved greatly. The stronger the shoulder, arm, and wrist muscles, the better able you are to execute and control the shot with the arm, rather than the legs. As a result, accuracy improves. Use your legs to get you airborne and create rhythm (as for a free throw or short jump shot). Use arm action, especially elbow extension and wrist flexion, to improve accuracy. These exercises increase strength

and groove the muscular pathway needed to execute the shot automatically. You develop the coordination needed to shoot quickly and accurately and, as a result, score more baskets. As you will see by looking at most of the shooting sequences in this chapter, higher-level players do not involve much shoulder flexion. They rely mostly on elbow extension and wrist flexion.

Biomechanical and Kinesiological Analysis of Basketball Shooting

Most shots in basketball consist of a jump, followed by the shoulder, arm, and wrist actions to propel the ball in an arc to the basket. The exact patterns of movement change with maturation and depend to a great extent on the strength and explosiveness of the muscles involved. The most successful shooters at an early age are those who have stronger legs to

Frame 1

Frame 2

Frame 3

Frame 4

Frame 5

Frame 6

Figure 5-4

get up higher and more arm and shoulder strength to shoot the ball.

By observing basketball players from the very early ages through the professional levels, you will notice that there is a definite progression in their shooting patterns. In essence, it goes from a *total-body push pattern*, to an *arm-push pattern* and then to an *arm-throw pattern*.

The Arm-Push Pattern

Most players use the arm-push pattern. In early youth, it is a double-leg push coupled with a double-arm push, executed simultaneously or with considerable overlap (Figure 5-1).

As strength increases and the player matures, the arm-push pattern becomes the best way to execute a shot. Exactly how it is executed, however, is often misunderstood. Because of this, it is not surprising to see various descriptions of the shot.

In effective technique, the ball is brought up in both hands until it is slightly above eye level or above the head. As you do this, the ball is turned around so that the shooting hand is now directly behind the ball, and the support hand is on the side of the ball. (See the first few frames of Figures 5-2 through 5-5.)

The elbow should be bent and pointed toward the basket (Figure 5-6, frame 3; Figure 5-7, frame 5; Figure 5-8, frames 1 through 5; Figure 5-9, frames 1 and 2). Note that in these figures the elbow is not always directly pointed towards the target. In each case, however, the ball is basically in the same position and directly above the head. It appears that the ball and the eye are lined up with the basket, but not necessarily the elbow. This is especially true when the player appears to have a *chicken wing* (Figure 5-10, frames 4 and 5). Ideally, it is advantageous to have the elbow in line with the basket. But in order to do this, the shooter must have more of a side-facing position. If he is square

Frame 7

Frame 8

Frame 9

Frame 10

Frame 11

Frame 12

Figure 5-4 (cont'd)

Frame 1

Frame 2

Frame 3

Frame 4

Frame 5

Frame 6

Frame 7

Frame 8

Frame 9

Frame 10

Frame 11

Frame 12

Figure 5-5

to the basket when he executes the jump shot or when he is getting ready to shoot, it is almost impossible to get the elbow pointed directly in front with the forearm up and wrist back. The shoulders will not allow it. But if you turn the shoulders so that the shooting arm shoulder is slightly in front, the elbow can be directed more toward the basket.

Even though the *chicken wing* position is considered to be a major fault in shooting (Figure 5-10, frames 3 through 6), it does not appear to be as serious as often believed. The key factor is that the elbow moves in during the execution of the shot so that at the moment of release, or just prior to release, the elbow, hand, and ball line up directly with the basket. This can be seen in each of the noted figures.

When ready to shoot, the arm action is as follows. There is initial elevation in the shoulder joint to raise the arm until the ball is slightly or completely above the head. The arm remains basically in place

Frame 1

Frame 2

Frame 3

Frame 4

Frame 5

Frame 6

Frame 7

Frame 8

Figure 5-6

Frame 1

Frame 2

Frame 3

Frame 4

Frame 5

Frame 6

Frame 7

Frame 8

Frame 9

Frame 10

Frame 11

Frame 12

Figure 5-7

as the elbow extension begins and the hand moves in a straight line toward the basket (Figure 5-2, frames 3 through 7; Figure 5-4, frames 4 through 6; Figure 5-11, frames 3 through 6; Figure 5-12, frames 3 through 6; Figure 5-13, frames 2 through 5). As the elbow approaches a 90-degree angle, there is additional shoulder flexion (the arm is raised higher). When combined with the continuing elbow extension, the arm straightens and wrist flexion takes place (Figures 5-2 through 5-5; Figure 5-11, frames 4 through 8; Figure 5-12, frames 5 through 7; Figure 5-13, frames 4 through 6; Figures 5-14, frames 6 through 9; Figure 5-15, frames 5 through 8).

The ball is pushed in the intended line of flight and aimed higher than the basket to put the ball on an arc into the basket. The higher the trajectory of the arc, the better the chances of the ball going through the hoop. As the shot trajectory flattens, the chances of success are reduced. This is why the arm rises before elbow extension concludes and the wrist flexion begins. This action puts the ball on a higher trajectory (arc) to the basket.

More specifically, there is flexion in the shoulder joint. The upper arm is raised, together with extension in the elbow joint to straighten the arm. These actions overlap to move the hand in a straight line toward the basket. These actions and the straight-line hand movement comprise a push pattern conducive to accuracy. All the force is directed in straight line, and the ball travels in an arc.

The muscles involved in the push pattern of shooting are as follows. In shoulder flexion (arm raising), the anterior and middle deltoid and the upper portion of the pectoralis major are the major muscles involved. The deltoid covers the front, side, and rear of the shoulder, but only the front and middle sections are involved. The upper clavicular portion of the pectoralis major covers the upper chest. In straightening the arm (elbow extension), the main muscle involved is the triceps brachii located on the back of the upper arm. The major muscles involved in wrist flexion – the last action in shooting – are the flexor carpi radialis, and the flexor carpi ulnaris located on the front of the forearm.

Frame 1

Frame 2

Frame 3

Frame 4

Frame 5

Frame 6

Frame 7

Figure 5-8

In wrist-joint flexion, the fingers stay basically in line with the hand, as the hand moves from a hyperextended position to form a straight line with the forearm, at which time the ball leaves the hand. After the ball is released, the hand continues moving forward and down (increased wrist flexion). In the follow-through, you see the wrist-flexed position. However, only the range of action from the hyperextended wrist position (which is needed to support the ball) to the straight hand-arm position is used to impart force and spin to the ball (Figures 5-2 through 5-5; Figure 5-11, frames 7 through 10; Figure 5-12, frames 3 through 8; Figure 5-13, frames 3 through 7; Figure 5-14, frames 6 through 10; Figure 5-15, frames 5 through 11).

The Arm-Throw Pattern

The arm-throw pattern of shooting involves three joints to create the power needed to push the ball far enough to reach the basket. In the throwing type shot, you rely on two joint actions — elbow extension and wrist flexion — increasing accuracy and preventing the shot from being blocked.

This shooting pattern evolved as the height of players increased and the game got faster. Defensive players were able to block push-pattern shots, mainly because the ball was in front of the head or directly above the head. To avoid having their shots blocked, many players began raising the ball higher and bringing the ball back behind the head so that it could not be touched by an opponent. The shooting elbow was raised as a result of holding the ball above and behind the head. This type of shooting relies more on a kinesthetic sense that is developed from increased strength and plenty of practice, linked with the vision to develop the correct ball pathway to the basket (Figure 5-16).

In execution of this shot, the elbow remains in place. The shooter relies on elbow extension and wrist flexion. The arc of the ball is slightly higher, which is conducive to greater accuracy. To execute this pattern of shooting, you need greater strength,

Frame 1

Frame 2

Frame 3

Frame 4

Frame 5

Figure 5-9

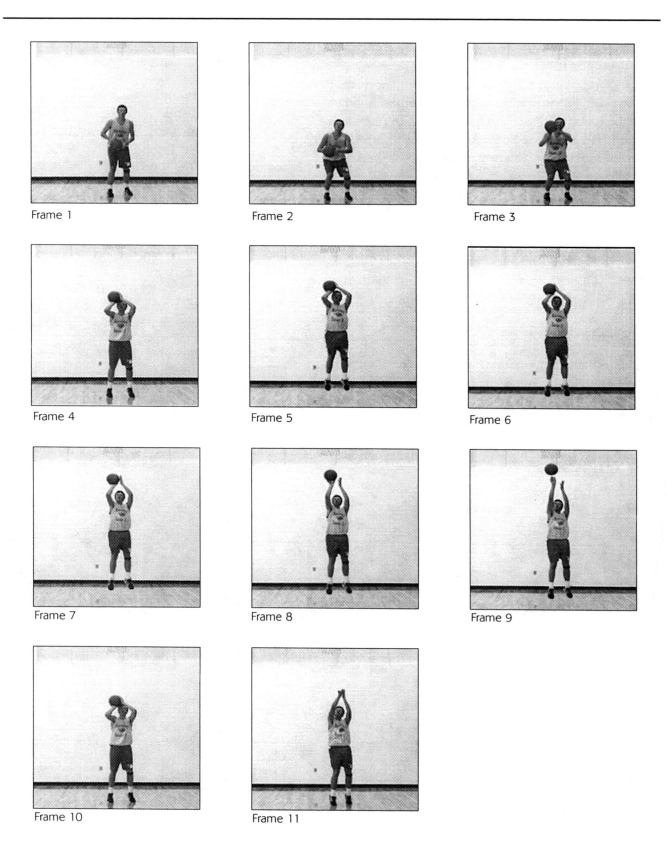

Frame 1

Frame 2

Frame 3

Frame 4

Frame 5

Frame 6

Frame 7

Frame 8

Frame 9

Frame 10

Frame 11

Figure 5-10

Frame 1

Frame 2

Frame 3

Frame 4

Frame 5

Frame 6

Frame 7

Frame 8

Frame 9

Frame 10

Figure 5-11

especially of the triceps for elbow extension and wrist flexor muscles to add power and accuracy. Some of the best professional and collegiate players use this pattern when executing two-point shots and some three-pointers. Other players with less strength use a combination of both shooting patterns, but rely mainly on elbow extension and wrist flexion to get the distance needed.

If you look carefully at Figures 5-2 through 5-5 and Figures 5-11 through 5-15, and compare them with Figure 5-16, you will see there is little difference between these shooting patterns. In both cases, when using the push pattern with the elbow held in place, or when the elbow is held up high as in the throw pattern, the ending position is basically the same. The ball is released in basically the same

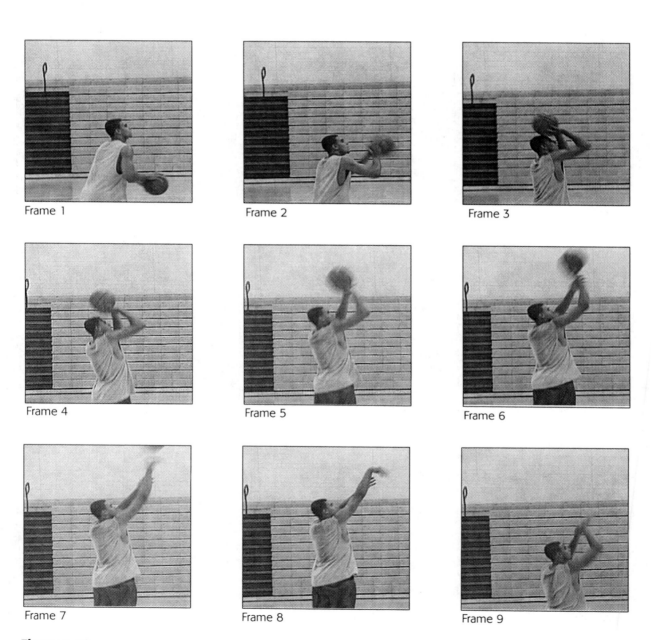

Frame 1

Frame 2

Frame 3

Frame 4

Frame 5

Frame 6

Frame 7

Frame 8

Frame 9

Figure 5-12

position regardless of the pattern being used. The major difference is that in the throw pattern the elbow is held higher initially. In the push pattern, the elbow is held lower and comes up prior to the ball being released.

Thus, there is not a major difference between these shooting patterns. The major advantage of the throw pattern is that it can help avoid having the shot blocked because of the initial positioning of the ball behind the body, as well as the higher arc trajectory. In all cases the ball is released when it is slightly in front of the body.

Combining the Jump with the Shooting Pattern

When executing the jump shot or simply a jump followed by a shot, regardless of the shooting pattern, the shot is executed in basically the same manner. If you look at the jump shot from a standing position (Figures 5-2 through 5-10), you can see how, in all cases, the ball is brought up overhead as the player prepares for the jump. Once the ball is

head-high or above the head, the actual jump begins. Full leg extension and takeoff occur prior to the actual shot being executed. In almost all cases, the ball is released close to the top of the jump.

The same holds true when executing a jump shot from a front approach (Figures 3-1, 3-2, and 3-3 in Chapter 3; Figures 5-14, 5-15, and 5-17 through 5-19 in this chapter). The ball is brought up head high or above as the leg extension and jump begins to take place. When the player is airborne, the ball is above the head. The shot begins at or near the top positions. The ball is released prior to descent.

The basic execution from a standing position, off the dribble or with an approach run is basically the same. However, as you move further away, the shot is executed slightly faster, especially the takeoff, because of the momentum generated by the approach. This can be seen in Figure 3-6, which was a three-point shot, as opposed to Figure 3-2, which was close to the free-throw line.

Frame 1

Frame 2

Frame 3

Frame 4

Frame 5

Frame 6

Frame 7

Frame 8

Figure 5-13

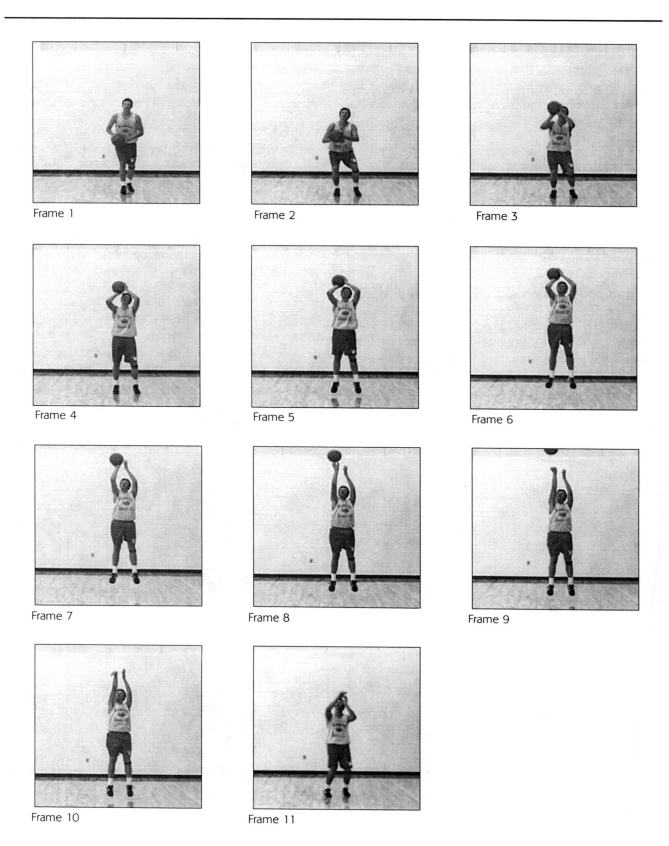

Frame 1

Frame 2

Frame 3

Frame 4

Frame 5

Frame 6

Frame 7

Frame 8

Frame 9

Frame 10

Frame 11

Figure 5-14

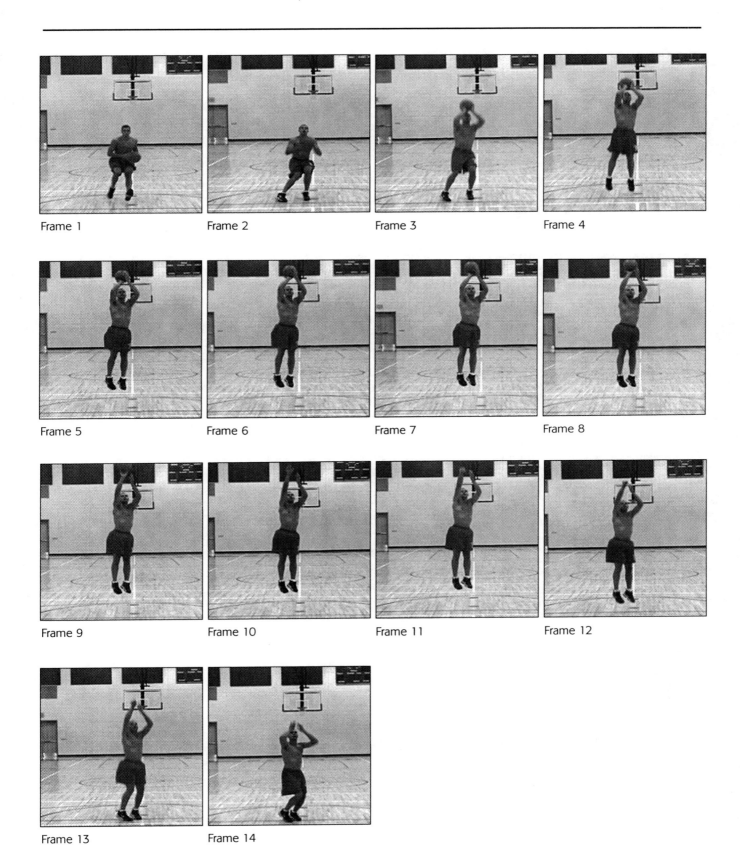

Frame 1   Frame 2   Frame 3   Frame 4

Frame 5   Frame 6   Frame 7   Frame 8

Frame 9   Frame 10   Frame 11   Frame 12

Frame 13   Frame 14

Figure 5-15

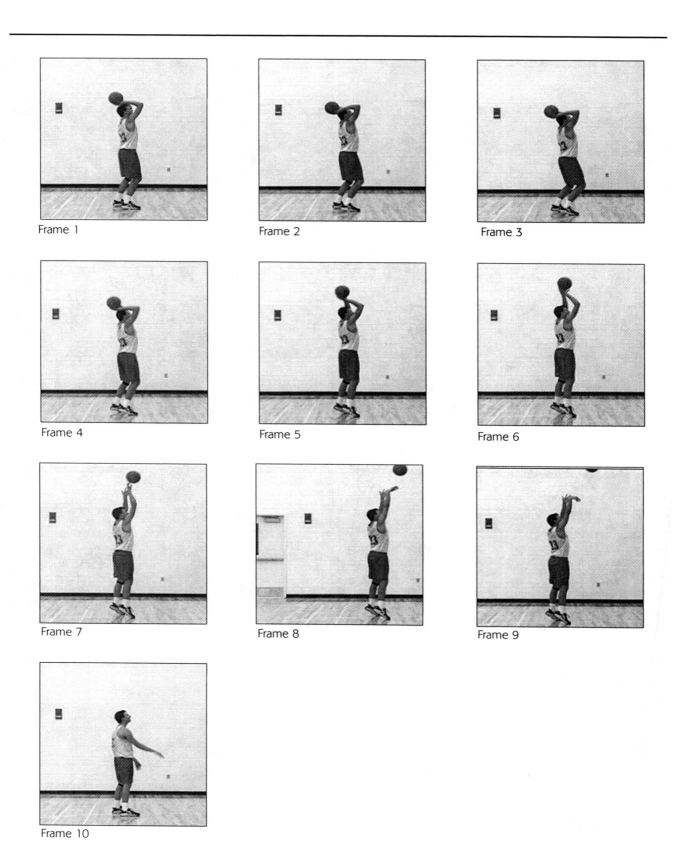

Frame 1

Frame 2

Frame 3

Frame 4

Frame 5

Frame 6

Frame 7

Frame 8

Frame 9

Frame 10

Figure 5-16

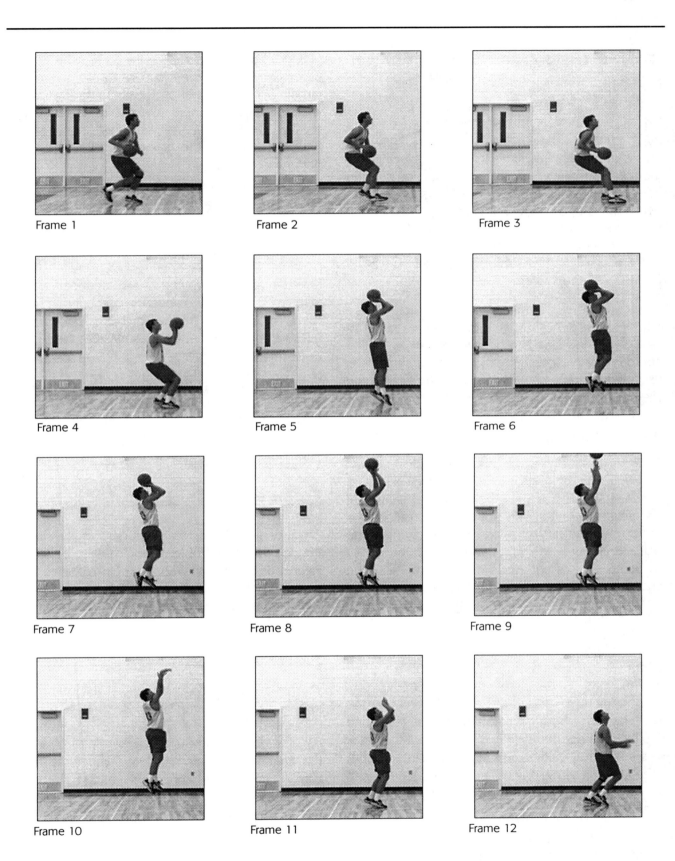

Frame 1

Frame 2

Frame 3

Frame 4

Frame 5

Frame 6

Frame 7

Frame 8

Frame 9

Frame 10

Frame 11

Frame 12

Figure 5-17

Double-Leg Jump Approach Followed by the Shot

Using the double-leg approach (taking off on one leg, leaping through the air, and landing on both legs, followed immediately by a jump upward) entails essentially the same pattern for execution of the shot. In Figures 5-17 through 5-19, you can see how the ball is brought up overhead as the legs are being straightened. The ball is already overhead at the moment of takeoff, and the shot is executed at the peak of the jump (Figure 5-17, frames 7 through 9; Figure 5-18, frames 7 through 9; and Figure 5-19, frames 10 through 12).

In Figures 5-17 and 5-18, it is possible to see that the player does not go into as deep a squat as he does in the standing position or with a regular approach before executing the jump. The takeoff is executed faster when using the double-leg jump method.

Body Positioning

Coaches routinely tell players to *square up* when shooting. This is a bit of a misnomer, or at least a misunderstanding. A frame-by-frame examination of shooting reveals that truly squared-up positioning is not biomechanically effective. In order to have the ball and elbow in line with the basket, it's necessary to stand at a slight angle to the rim, with the shooting arm in front and the ball directly over the head, but more on the side of the shooting arm.

If you are right-handed shooter, the ball lines up more or less with the right eye and the right elbow (Figure 5-8, frames 3 through 7; Figure 5-9, frames 1 through 5; Figure 5-15, frames 4 through 10). Also notice in Figures 5-8, 5-9, and 5-15 that the shooting-arm elbow is pointed toward the target and the ball is positioned slightly to the right of the head. The support or guiding arm elbow is pointed out to the side. This is necessary to maintain contact with the ball and have the other elbow pointed toward the target.

If you hold the ball with the shooting elbow pointing out to the side, the support elbow will be pointed more or less toward the target. This is what occurs when you have a square stance toward the target (Figures 5-10 and 5-14). To keep the shooting elbow pointed toward the target, use a slightly sideways stance with the shooting arm toward the basket. This gives you better vision and better mechanics.

Speed of Execution

(Note: Most of the pictures in this section were taken at a high shutter speed to show the exact positioning of the limbs during the jump and shot. A few sequences were shot at regular speed to give some indication of the speed of execution. In these cases, you will see the ball or limbs looking fuzzy because the movement was too fast for the camera to catch a clear picture.)

In Figure 5-12, the ball is brought up from frames 1 to 2 fairly rapidly until the ball is directly over the head. During the jump and the beginning of the shot from frames 4 through 5, the ball again gets fuzzy. As the shot proceeds to the elbow extension and the elbow rises in the push pattern, we see the speed of the ball increasing so that, at the moment of release, the ball and hand are a blur.

The hand becomes clear only in the follow-through. The speed of execution can also be seen in Figures 3-2, 3-6, and 5-2. The ball becomes fuzzy, or does not have a clear outline during the shot execution when it is initially brought up into position for the shot.

The Lay-up

The key to successful execution of the lay-up is to jump sufficiently high. There is no true shooting pattern involved, since it is a matter of raising the ball and lifting it up into the basket or banking it off the backboard. In some cases, especially if the player cannot rise above the basket, he must execute essentially the same type of shot as described previously. For example, in Figure 5-20, you can see both hands on the ball with the ball above the head – but more in front than in the usual

Frame 1

Frame 2

Frame 3

Frame 4

Frame 5

Frame 6

Frame 7

Frame 8

Frame 9

Frame 10

Figure 5-18

Frame 1

Frame 2

Frame 3

Frame 4

Frame 5

Frame 6

Frame 7

Frame 8

Frame 9

Frame 10

Frame 11

Frame 12

Frame 13

Frame 14

Frame 15

Figure 5-19

Frame 1

Frame 2

Frame 3

Frame 4

Frame 5

Frame 6

Frame 7

Frame 8

Frame 9

Frame 10

Frame 11

Frame 12

Figure 5-20

jump shot. During execution, the elbow extends and is raised, followed by slight wrist flexion.

If the jump is sufficiently high, the arm straightens to increase the height of the ball at release, and there is no wrist flexion. In this case, the hand remains in line with the forearm. In some cases, it's laid back into hyperextension to allow the ball to roll off the fingers up and into the basket or backboard. The ball is given its force at the takeoff and as the guiding hand releases it. The shooting hand carries and directs the ball, rather than supplying a major force to get the ball up into the target area (Figures 3-14, 3-15, and 5-21).

The biggest difference is in the jump, which is a one-legged takeoff, as opposed to a double-legged takeoff as in the other shots (Figures 3-14; 3-15, frames 2 through 4; and 5-21). See Chapter 3 for more information on the jump takeoff involved in the lay-up.

The Tip-In

There are many variations of the tip-in. Each depends on where the body and ball are when you meet the ball. For example, if the ball has some speed, as during the rebound, you may first catch it in two hands and then execute the one-handed shot as previously described. An example of this is seen in Figure 5-22. In some cases, if the ball is off to one side, it becomes impossible to catch the ball in both hands. Thus, you must reach the ball in one hand, cushion it somewhat, and then execute either a wrist flick or elbow extension if the ball is sufficiently low. If you are fully extended to reach the ball, it becomes a matter of using only the wrist to bring the ball back up and over the basket (Figure 5-23).

Use of Heavier and Lighter Balls

One final point about improving range and accuracy: the use of heavier and lighter balls in practice help

Frame 1

Frame 2

Frame 3

Frame 4

Frame 5

Frame 6

Figure 5-21

to improve shooting. Integrated with regulation-weight balls, different-weight balls can improve shooting range and quickness of release. This is important when the defense is contesting your shot.

Players should use these heavier and lighter balls in a particular pattern to work on their jump shots. They will be able to shoot further and feel more confident in getting the shot off, especially when closely guarded. The heavier and lighter balls also improve speed and power in passing, and are useful in various dribbling drills.

(For more information on the weighted balls and how they can be used, contact Sports Training Inc., P. O. Box 92046, Escondido, California 92046, 760-480-0558, or visit website: http://www.dryessis.com.)

Frame 1

Frame 2

Frame 3

Frame 4

Frame 5

Frame 6

Frame 7

Frame 8

Frame 9

Figure 5-22

Frame 1

Frame 2

Frame 3

Frame 4

Frame 5

Frame 6

Frame 7

Frame 8

Frame 9

Figure 5-23

CHAPTER 6

Specialized Exercises for Shooting

As was stated in the previous chapter, strength is a critical (and misunderstood) element of shooting a basketball. It is possible to develop the strength needed to improve shooting technique, range, and accuracy. If you're looking to make a marked improvement in your shooting, incorporate some or all of the following 10 exercises into your workout routine. Most of these exercises duplicate the joint actions involved in shooting.

The Bench Press

When executed with the elbows alongside the body, the bench press duplicates the basic arm-push pattern seen in shooting. The actions in the elbow and shoulder joint are basically the same, although

the sequence of use is slightly different. Regardless, you strengthen the major muscles involved in a balanced manner.

Execution: Assume a face-up prone position on an exercise bench, holding a barbell or dumbbells with a neutral grip and with the arms fully extended above the chest. When ready, inhale and hold your breath as you lower the dumbbells (or bar), keeping the elbows in close so they pass the sides of the body and go below the level of the body. As the dumbbells approach the level of the chest, keep holding your breath. Then reverse direction and push the weights back up to the straight-arm position. Exhale as you pass the most difficult point on the up phase, and pause momentarily after

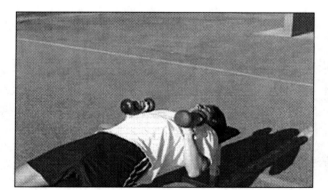

Figure 6-1a

Figure 6-1b

Figure 6-1c

Figure 6-1d

reaching the straight-arm position. Repeat when ready (Figures 6-1a and 6-1b).

You should also do the bench press with a pronated grip, with your elbows pointed out to the side to prevent shoulder injury and to attain more powerful arm actions for passing the ball. Use a barbell or dumbbells and execute the same as when using the neutral grip. The only difference is the elbows remain pointed outward throughout execution (Figures 6-1c and 6-1d).

The Lying 45-Degree Triceps Extension

This exercise duplicates the ideal throwing pattern. More specifically, it duplicates the angle seen in the shoulder joint and elbow joint when shooting in the push or throw pattern. If you hold the elbow or the upper arm about 10 to 20 degrees above the horizontal when executing the shot, you should hold the arm in basically the same position when doing the triceps extension exercise. If you use a basic throw pattern with the arm held at approximately a 45-degree angle to the horizontal, this is the angle you should hold during this strength exercise.

Execution: Assume a face-up supine position on a bench, holding a barbell or dumbbells in the hands. In assuming your position, keep the arms vertical and hold the dumbbells (or barbell) above in a balanced position. When ready, bend the elbows 90 degrees. As you bring the elbows back beyond the head 10 or more degrees (depending on the angle used in your shot), hold the elbows in position. Then straighten the arms to full extension. Return to the bent-elbow position, being sure to hold the elbow in position at all times.

Do not move the elbow to the vertical position (which makes the exercise easier but also defeats the purpose of the exercise). Inhale and hold your breath as you execute the elbow extension and as you return to the initial position. Quickly exhale, then inhale and repeat (Figures 6-2a through 6-2c).

Forearm Pronation and Supination

Pronation of the shooting-arm forearm occurs in the final stages of the preparation for the shot and after the release. The shooting hand pronates to get behind the ball while the guiding (support) hand

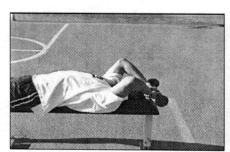

Figure 6-2a

Figure 6-2b

Figure 6-2c

supinates to get the ball in good position. (Pronation can also be seen when executing a pass, while supination is needed when catching or grabbing a ball and bringing it in close to the body.)

Forearm pronation can be done separately, or it can be combined with forearm supination in one exercise to provide full forearm development. To ensure balanced development of the forearm muscles, supination and pronation will be described in one exercise.

Execution: Kneel in front of the long side of an exercise bench and place one forearm across the bench seat so that your wrist and hand are clear of the seat. Hold a Strength Bar (see Figure 6-3) in your hand in a neutral grip—i.e., with your thumb in the uppermost position, the bar vertical, and the weight at the top end. When ready, turn your hand palm up (supinate) until the shaft of the bar is almost level or in line with the bench. The weighted end should point outward. Be sure to keep your forearm in contact with the bench as you do this action.

Then turn the hand palm down (pronate) so that the bar is once again vertical. Go beyond (additional pronation) until the bar is once again level to the bench. In this way, you execute supination and pronation through a full 180 degrees ROM. After reaching the lowermost position, turn the palm up again, maintaining continuous motion to the right and the left at a moderate rate of speed (Figure 6-3a through 6-3c). Repeat with the other arm so that you do not overdevelop the muscles of only one arm. Keep your shoulder over your elbow to maintain a 90-degree angle in the elbow at all times, and so the elbow remains in contact with the bench.

Note that doing pronation and supination with a dumbbell is not effective because the resistance lever arm is too short. In essence, the closer the resistance to the hand, the easier it is to turn your hand and the less the muscular development that will occur. When you use the Strength Bar, you can adjust the length of the lever by holding the weighted end closer to or farther from your hand.

Figure 6-3a

Figure 6-3b

Figure 6-3c

Triceps Extension (Triceps Push Down)

This exercise is important for all shots, but especially for the arm-throw pattern of shooting.

Execution: Stand in front of a high cable pulley machine or a high attachment of the rubber tubing. Grasp the handle with a pronated grip and with the elbows close to the sides of the body. When ready, inhale and hold your breath, as you push down with the hands until the arms are fully extended (straight). Hold for one to two seconds. Keep the elbows alongside the body at all times. Exhale as you return to the initial position, and inhale and hold as you repeat. Start with the hands above the elbows and keep the hands in line with the forearms at all times (Figures 6-4a through 6-4d).

French Press (Overhead Elbow Extension)

This exercise strengthens the triceps muscle in elbow extension with the arm in an overhead position. It develops strength needed during tip-ins, actions around the basket, and when fighting for the ball. While it does not duplicate the total shooting action, with some modification it is a good exercise for strengthening the triceps muscle for shooting actions.

Execution: Assume a comfortable standing position, holding a dumbbell in one hand. Raise the arm overhead so that the elbow is pointed upward at an angle of 45 to 60 degrees, with the elbow bent and the weight behind the body (Figure 6-5a). When ready, inhale and hold your breath as you fully extend the arm until it is completely straight (Figure 6-5b). Exhale and return to the initial position under control. Repeat at a moderate rate of speed.

Wrist Curls

This exercise strengthens the wrist-flexor muscles needed in releasing the ball in most shots. It is also a good exercise for overall strengthening of the wrists.

Execution: Assume a kneeling position in front of an exercise bench, with the forearms on the bench seat. The wrists and hands should hang beyond the bench and be free to move through a full range of motion. Hold a barbell, Strength Bar, or dumbbells in the hands. When ready, lower the hands as far as possible with a relaxed grip. Then raise the hand (and weights) as far as possible while keeping the forearms in contact with the bench. Return to the down position under control and repeat. Go through 120 to 140 degrees of motion (Figures 6-6a through 6-6c).

Be sure to fully hyperextend the wrists on the down-phase, so that you start the exercise basically in the position the hand is in when beginning to execute a shot. Duplicate the range from the hyperextended position to the neutral position

Figure 6-4a

Figure 6-4b

Figure 6-4c

Figure 6-4d

when the hand is in line with the forearm. To balance the wrist flexor muscle strength, do reverse wrist curls. Execution is the same as wrist curls except the palms face downward (Figure 6-6c).

Finger Exercises

The fingers play an extremely important role in gripping and releasing the ball. Some players are more successful in gripping the ball because of their ability to spread the fingers sufficiently to cover most of the ball. Once you develop the fingers you can grip, shoot, and pass the ball more effectively, even when your hands and fingers are not as big as other players'.

Finger exercises should be done with ExerRings, which consist of six rings of different tensions, three of which are round with rounded surfaces, and three of which are round but with flat outer surfaces. The round surface is used more for gripping and finger flexion, while the flat surface allows for better fingertip contact to work each digit

Figure 6-5a

Figure 6-5b

individually or to work extended fingers. The flat surface ring is also beneficial for finger adduction and abduction.

Execution: To develop finger flexion strength as needed in gripping, select a round ring with the needed tension. Place the ring against the middle pads of your fingers and the base of the thumb and palm. When ready, squeeze the ring maximally so that in the ending position your hand is in a fist. The ring at this time should be in the shape of a figure eight. After strongly contracting the finger muscles, relax your grip until the ring resumes its round shape. Repeat for the desired number of repetitions. Change the positioning of the ring on the fingers for different effects (Figures 6-7a and 6-7b).

To work the fingers when they are fully extended, as they are during the last split second before the ball leaves the fingers, grasp the flat ring with the fingertips. Place the thumb on a tabletop or on your thigh, then press down with the fingertips. After the ring is fully deformed into the shape of a figure eight, relax the muscles to return the ring to its original normal shape. For more precision, isolate the action to the index and middle fingers (Figures 6-8a and 6-8b).

Wrist Flick with a Medicine Ball

In all shots, the wrist goes from a hyperextended position to the neutral position as the ball is released. The ball actually leaves the index and middle finger last as they impart spin to the ball. This action must be fairly forceful to impart greater speed to the ball and to give it sufficient spin, which helps to control its flight through the air.

Execution: Assume a face-up prone position on an exercise bench, holding the shooting arm up with the elbow bent. The elbow is pointed directly upward and the forearm is laid back and basically horizontal or parallel with the floor or bench (Figure 6-9). Select a small medicine ball (one to two pounds). When ready, toss the ball up with a flick of the wrist approximately 12 inches. Catch the ball as it comes down, reassume the position, and then

Figure 6-6a

Figure 6-6b

Figure 6-6c

Explosive-Wrist Flick with a Medicine Ball

In many instances, such as a quick shot or tip-in, you'll use only one hand to shoot. To improve this quick action, do the explosive-wrist flick. You'll need a partner for this exercise.

Execution: Assume the same position as in the regular wrist flick. Your partner should stand over you, holding a small light medicine ball (one to two pounds) directly above your hand. When ready, your partner releases the ball, and you catch and toss the ball back up in one motion. Your partner

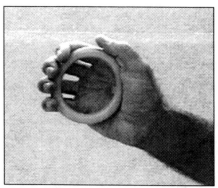

Figure 6-7a

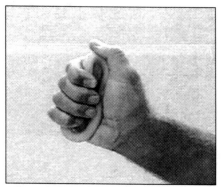

Figure 6-7b

flick the ball back up again. You will notice that as you do this there will also be some elbow-joint extension. Both of these actions occur in the shot. This exercise develops greater strength of the wrist flexors and the ability to get a quicker wrist-action release.

then catches the ball, you re-assume the position, and when you are ready he once again releases the ball and you catch and toss it back up as quickly as possible. In this way you develop the ability to use a quick wrist action to execute a tip-in or another play action (Figures 6-10a through 6-10c).

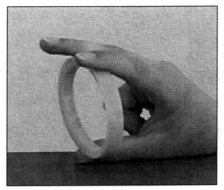

Figure 6-8a

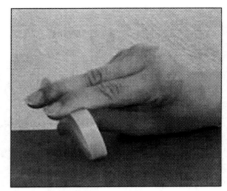

Figure 6-8b

Front-Arm Raises

This exercise is important for raising the ball upward to get it in an overhead position as you jump up to execute the shot, as well as to strengthen the muscles involved in raising the elbow during the push-pattern shot execution.

Execution: Assume a standing position, holding a dumbbell in each hand. Hold the dumbbells with a neutral grip so that the shaft of the dumbbell runs forward and backward. When ready, inhale and hold your breath as you raise the arms straight up until they are completely overhead. This full range of motion is needed to ensure maximum flexibility in

Figure 6-9a

Figure 6-9b

Figure 6-9c

Figure 6-9d

Figure 6-9e

 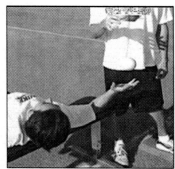 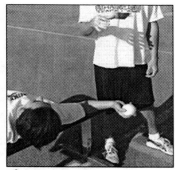

Figure 6-10a   Figure 6-10b   Figure 6-10c

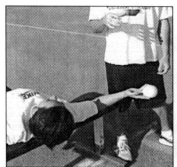   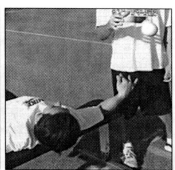

Figure 6-10d   Figure 6-10e   Figure 6-10f   Figure 6-10g

the shoulder joint while developing strength through the entire range of motion. Exhale and return to the initial position under control and repeat (Figure 6-11a and 6-11b).

To duplicate the strength needed in raising the ball overhead and to hold the arm position seen in shooting, do the exercise by raising the arms upward until they are overhead, or up to about a 45-degree position. If you know the exact angle at which you hold the elbow during shooting, raise the arm to that position and hold for two to three seconds to develop the isometric strength needed to maintain a stable arm position. After holding, return to the initial position and repeat (Figure 6-11a through 6-11c).

Figure 6-11a   Figure 6-11b   Figure 6-11c

CHAPTER 7

Techniques for Improving Running Speed

Running speed, the ability to get from *Point A to Point B* in as little time as possible, is an important predictor of athletic success. All things being equal, the faster athlete in almost any sport has a significant advantage over slower athletes. Basketball is no exception to the rule.

Basketball coaches and trainers understand this fundamental principle, and attempt to improve athletes' speed by a variety of methods, ranging from useful, to ineffective, to potentially counter-productive or even injurious. For instance, the prevalent philosophy seems to be — *do more running*. Its practitioners strongly believe that by doing more running, especially on an intense level, athletes improve speed and conditioning. This is why many basketball players only run before and/or after playing and do so on a year-round basis, as opposed to doing supplementary strength and sprint training. And this is also why so many players suffer injuries while running or playing.

Too many coaches, trainers, and players focus on the *quantity* of running, as opposed to its *quality*. By reversing this approach and concentrating on quality, athletes can develop flat-out speed and endurance, while reducing the likelihood of injury.

Changes in running technique and efficiency are easy to make. The greater an athlete's neuromuscular skill and raw physical abilities, the easier it is to make changes. For example, most of the basketball players shown in this book were able to pick up changes very quickly. They were all good players and had the necessary strength and coordination. After a few repetitions, they were able to pick it up, and it soon became second nature to them. The key point here is that you can change technique to make your running (and other basketball skills) more economical and mechanically sound. By improving your physical qualities, you can make these changes more easily, quickly, and effectively.

Through biomechanics and kinesiology, it's possible to determine what constitutes good running technique, and why such technique is effective. In essence, you learn the best way to run, and why it is the best way to run for basketball. You also learn how effective running helps prevent injury.

Biomechanics and kinesiology can improve running and overall performance through the analysis and understanding of each of the main elements (actions) involved in running, and how they are executed. Once effective technique or

Frame 1

Frame 2

Frame 3

Frame 4

Frame 5

Frame 6

Frame 7

Frame 8

Frame 9

Frame 10

Frame 11

Frame 12

Figure 7-1

execution of the key joint actions is known, it's possible to create exercises that duplicate these exact movements. In this way, gains in strength, flexibility, and other physical factors have a more direct and immediate impact on running speed. Knowing the muscles that are involved and how they are involved in each joint action makes it easier to create effective exercises.

Running Specifics

It's hard to find a basketball player with perfect running technique. (For that matter, perfect running technique is rare even among the world-class runners.) In basketball, most elite-level players have strong positive aspects to their running techniques. These pluses enable them to outrun opponents up and down the court.

The photos in this book feature some excellent basketball players. However, no single photo or athlete illustrates every positive aspect of the most effective technique for sprinting down the court.

When referring to particular figures, examine the frames in question for the positive or well-executed portions of the technique. Know that other aspects of each athlete's technique may be improved.

For effective running technique in basketball, it's not necessary to duplicate the best technique of a world-class sprinter. Most important in basketball is the ability to execute quick bursts of speed to get by an opponent, or to run a fast break. Also important is the ability to run effectively for an entire game without undue fatigue.

To achieve greater speed and prevent early fatigue, it is important to have effective technique. The better the technique, the easier and more economical it is to run. This not only gets you from one point to another faster, but also allows you to do it more often, without unnecessary fatigue. Keep in mind that the more economical your running, the less fatigued you become and the more capable you are of executing a good jump shot or some defensive play after the run.

Frame 13

Frame 14

Frame 15

Frame 16

Frame 17

Figure 7-1 (cont'd)

In the following biomechanical analysis of running technique, some of the key aspects are reviewed that you can incorporate to make you faster with the least amount of effort. These are techniques that have been developed over years of working with many players. These techniques enabled them to become better players.

Running technique is broken down into three phases, each of which will be discussed and illustrated at length in this chapter. These phases are: *Push-Off, Flight,* and *Support.* Proper execution of each of these phases is a major key to increasing speed.

The *Push-Off* phase creates greater horizontal force for speed and gets the athlete airborne (Figure 7-1, frames 1 through 3 and 8 through 11; Figure 7-2, frame 2; Figure 7-3, frames 1 and 2). In the *Flight phase,* the athlete uses forces generated in the Push-Off to cover the optimal, but not maximal distance, and to prepare for touchdown (Figure 7-1, frames 3 through 6; Figure 7-2, frames 3 through 5). *The Support* phase, which occurs as soon as the foot makes contact with the ground, supports the body while minimizing up-and-down motions (Figure 7-1, frames 7 and 8; Figure 7-2, frame 1; Figure 7-3, frames 4 and 5).

The Push-Off Phase

The Push-Off phase involves one major joint action: ankle extension. The more powerful the ankle-joint extension is, the greater the forward driving force you can generate.

If the Push-Off (support) leg straightens fully, the athlete is leaping, not running. Straightening the leg fully gives more of a vertical—force component (as opposed to horizontal). The more horizontal the force, the faster the speed. In addition, full-leg extension requires more energy, which is wasted on up and down motion. As the ankle extension takes place, the knee of the athlete's Push-Off leg should remain slightly bent.

Some knee extension takes place, but not primarily for forward propulsion. In some cases, it may contribute a small component to horizontal force. If leg extension were very forceful, the leg would fully straighten. But you can see how the leg does not fully extend in the best players (Figure 7-1, frames 2 through 3 and 10 through 12; Figure 7-2, frames 2 and 6; Figure 7-3, frames 1 and 5 through 7).

During Push-Off, the swing-leg thigh drives forward forcefully. There is full ankle-joint extension so that the athlete is on his *tiptoe.* An initial forceful contraction of the hip-flexor muscles (iliopsoas, pectineus, and rectus femoris) when the leg is behind the body (before the Push-Off) drives the swing-leg thigh through (Figure 7-1, frames 4 through 7; Figure 7-2, frames 3 through 5). The more forceful the initial muscular contraction, the higher the thigh will rise – usually 55 to 75 degrees in relation to the body (Figure 7-1, frames 2 and 11; Figure 7-2, frames 2 and 6).

Knee drive is a key force-producing action that contributes greatly to speed. This action consists of driving the knee or thigh forward, not upward. To prepare for touchdown, the shin swings out to create a long lever, which slows the leg down (Figure 7-1, frames 2 through 5 and 10 through 14; Figure 7-2, frames 2 through 4). The straight leg is then used to create more force when it is driven down and back to make contact with the floor. This action entails use of the hamstring and gluteus maximus muscles (Figure 7-1, frames 5 through 7 and 14 through 17; Figure 7-2, frames 4 through 5 and 7 through 8).

To ensure the shortest lever possible, the athlete must raise the toe part of the foot when the shin swings out (Figure 7-1, frames 2 through 4 and 10 through 13; Figure 7-2, frames 5 and 6). This dorsi-flex action positions the leg more under the body in order to land on the ball of the foot or mid-foot. By keeping his toes pointed as they are after the Push-Off, the athlete takes longer to swing the leg out in front and make contacts with the ground earlier, well in front of the body instead of closer to the vertical projection of his center of gravity. Thus, the dorsi flexion plays an important role, not only to increase speed of movement of the shin, but also to ensure an effective landing. For most athletes this is a natural action.

The shin does not fold up completely behind the thigh. Most important is that the shin be behind the length of the thigh–between two perpendicular-to-the-thigh lines, drawn from the knee and the hip. The level (or slightly above level) position of the shin during the forward drive saves energy, as there is less need to contract the hamstring muscles (Figure 7-1, frames 4 through 8 and 13 through 17; Figure 7-2, frames 3 through 5).

Note also that the shin must be sufficiently above level so that the foot is *hidden* behind the length of the thigh. Because of the great rearward forces generated in the Push-Off, the heel rises higher, so that it comes close to the buttocks when the knee is in front of the body. When the heel nears the buttocks, but never touches it, the knee should be in front of the body (Figure 7-1, frames 8 and 9). This folding of the leg, coupled with the knee drive, is very safe. (Note: Touching the heel to the butt works the hamstrings when they should be relaxing. This leads to hamstring pulls. The "butt kick" also detracts from driving the thigh forward and, as a result, slows you down.)

The arm bends and moves forward in front of the body until the hand is about chest or shoulder high. The elbow bend approaches 90 degrees during the forward drive (Figure 7-1, frames 1 through 3; Figure 7-2, frames 1 and 2). When the arm moves backward, it straightens in preparation for touchdown (Figure 7-1, frames 6 through 8; Figure 7-2, frames 4 and 5). This action creates more force against the floor to produce a more powerful push-off. When dribbling, leg movements must be coordinated with the dribble to be in synchronization.

The Flight Phase

The Flight phase, also known as the airborne phase, is about as long as the Support phase. The more frequently the foot (leg) is in contact with the

Frame 1   Frame 2   Frame 3   Frame 4

Frame 5   Frame 6   Frame 7   Frame 8

Figure 7-2

ground, the more force it can generate for continual forward drive. There must be a Flight phase to use the force that has been generated in the Push-Off and knee-and-arm drive.

In the Flight phase, as the swing-leg thigh continues forward and reaches its highest point, the shin swings out and the thigh is stops (Figure 7-1, frames 2 through 4 and 10 through 14; Figure 7-2, frames 2 through 4). At this time, the leg begins movement downward and rearward in preparation for touchdown via powerful contractions of the hamstring muscles (Figure 7-1, frames 4 through 7 and 14 through 17; Figure 7-2, frames 4 and 5). This is where the hamstrings do their most important work.

When the foot contacts the floor and stops, the upper body continues to move forward. This major action of driving the leg down and back, known as *pawback*, contributes greatly to forward speed. In sprinting, the leg is brought back very forcefully so that

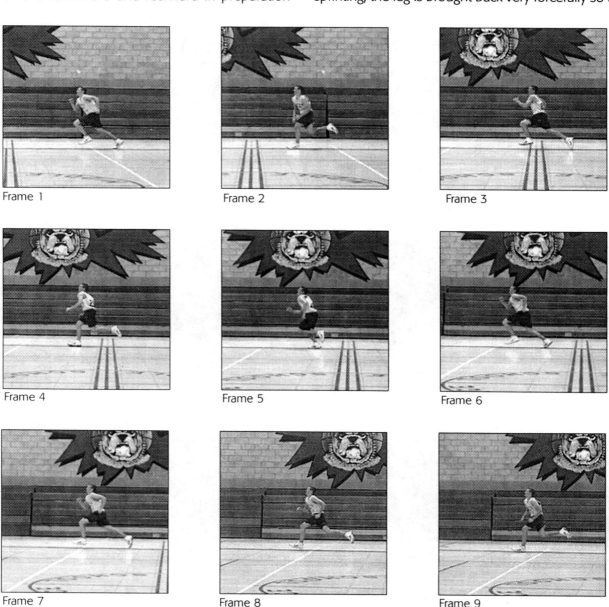

Frame 1

Frame 2

Frame 3

Frame 4

Frame 5

Frame 6

Frame 7

Frame 8

Frame 9

Figure 7-3

touchdown is directly under the body on the ball of the foot or ball-heel. When running slower, landing takes place slightly in front of the body on mid-foot or ball-heel (Figure 7-3, frames 8 through 9).

One of the most common problems I see among basketball players is a lack of pawback action. For example, look at Figure 7-3, frames 3 through 4 and 7 through 9. The player has a good Push-Off and knee drive. The knee is well out in front of the body. However, instead of swinging his shin leg out and back, he simply drops the leg straight down to make contact with the ground. When this happens, his trail leg is way behind his body. It then takes a long time to bring it forward for Push-Off. He gets no force out of the leg when it comes in contact with the ground. This slows him quite a bit. Not only does it act as a brake to his forward progress, he also doesn't get any additional force from the backward moving leg to propel the upper body forward.

Note his excessive forward lean during the run. Leaning forward should only be used when accelerating, not when in full stride. The closer the foot lands to the vertical projection of the body's center of mass (directly under the body), the less the braking forces. This is the main reason why the heel hit is so inefficient in running. Landing on your heel in front of your body momentarily stops your forward motion. These landing forces, which can be up to 10 times body weight, are the culprit in many leg, hip, and lower back injuries. To eliminate these braking forces as much as possible, it is important that the leg be moving backward as it makes contact with the ground.

The backward leg movement and the following touchdown are very important in continuing fast forward movement of the upper body. At floor contact, the upper body moves in front of the support leg so that when the Push-Off occurs, the body will be out in front as far as possible (Figure 7-1, frames 2 through 3 and 11 through 12). In this way the Push-Off is directed in a more horizontal forward line, rather than projecting the body upward as typically occurs in the heel hit.

Note that in the heel hit, when the whole foot comes down to make contact with the ground, it takes longer for the upper body to move over the foot. As a result, during Push-Off, the body is not as far forward as possible and has a very strong vertical Push-Off component. The heel hit precludes sprinting at top speed, and is highly dangerous because of the greater landing forces it generates.

This having been said, there is a time and place for the heel hit. In preparation for a jump shot off the run or dribble, the heel hit is very effective because of its stopping action. By fully extending the leg out in front and making contact with the ground on the heel, the athlete blocks, or stops, lower-body movement. The upper body continues moving forward until it is over the legs – the perfect time to extend the legs to jump upward. When running, you do not want the heel hit. Use it prior to executing a jump shot or to stop and change direction.

The Support Phase

The Support phase (Figure 7-1, frames 7 and 8; Figure 7-2, frame 1), also known as the amortization phase, begins when the foot makes contact with the floor. Technically, the Support phase ends when contact with the floor is broken at the end of the Push-Off. However, the body is in full support on the leg mainly when initial contact is made. The leg bends slightly to absorb some forces, and to withstand most of the forces needed for Push-Off. Half of Support time is for the landing, and half is for Push-Off.

The major Support phase is the landing, i.e., when the foot makes contact with the floor and the body's full weight is over the foot. The more up and down motion you have in running, the more energy you use, and the less efficient the run. If leg support muscles are weak and allow the athlete to *sink* too much after touchdown, he or she will consume extra energy, which can bring on early fatigue.

The following example shows how much energy may be expended over the course of a game. If you lift your body higher by one-quarter of an inch (one additional quarter-inch of vertical lift prior to each Push-Off), you do the equivalent of lifting your body mass to the height of a five-story building. Performed during a game, this extra work has a strong negative influence on running speed. The more horizontally your body moves in running, the greater your speed.

To prevent excessive flexion in the knee, the quadriceps muscle contracts eccentrically (it tenses as it lengthens) and then contracts isometrically to hold the leg position. If this muscle is weak, the result is excessive sinking of the body. Also, by not making contact close to mid-foot or on the ball of the foot, the foot and Achilles tendons will not be positioned to withstand any of the landing forces. They are very important for the initial shock absorption and for tensing the muscles and tendons on the plantar (under) surface of the foot. At the same time, ankle, knee, and hip joints undergo slight flexion to help absorb some of the landing forces and most importantly, to withstand the landing forces.

Stretching the Achilles and other tendons is important to create energy in the Push-Off. As the tendons are forcefully and quickly stretched, tension develops in the tendons (and associated muscles). The energy stored in this tension is used in the Push-Off. If all forces are absorbed, there is no energy to give back in the Push-Off. Thus, there should only be enough absorption to cushion the athlete and prevent injury on initial contact. Also, when landing on the heel, the Achilles tendon cannot absorb or withstand any of the landing forces. These forces travel up the body and become dangerous.

The Arm Actions

In effective and safe running, arm and leg actions must coordinate. When running slowly, the arms are held with approximately a 90-degree angle at the elbows to save energy. The elbow rises to the rear during the backswing phase of the arm action, while the opposite arm moves forward to synchronize

with the thigh drive. The elbow rises approximately 45 degrees to the rear, as it mimics the range of motion in the hip joint (Figure 7-1, frame 11; Figure 7-2, frame 7).

The arms should move in a forward/backward motion so that all the driving forces move in a straight line forward (Figure 7-4). If your shoulders rotate (turn sideways), the arms may appear to cross the body, but in reality they do not. If you see hands coming across the body, check to see if it is due to the shoulder rotation, or if elbows flare out to the sides. The player in Figure 7-4 has some rotation of the shoulders (compare frame 4 to frame 8) and moves his left arm across and out to the sides. These are inefficient actions. His right arm movement is basically good, but he does have some cross movements.

In sprinting, there should be a powerful forward drive of the arm as the elbow flexes to 90 degrees after being straightened on the backswing. The arm flexes and moves forward until the elbow is alongside or slightly in front of the body. There is approximately a 90-degree bend in the elbow, and the hand is between chest and shoulder height (Figure 7-1, frame 3; Figure 7-2, frame 2). The arm straightens as it moves back and down so that when the arm is alongside the body it is relatively straight (Figure 7-1, frame 8; Figure 7-2, frame 5). The long lever of the arm is needed to slow it down so that it synchronizes with the leg stopping when the foot is in contact with the ground.

After the arm straightens, the elbow rises to the rear. This action bends the elbow slightly and prepares it for being driven forward in synchronization with the bent leg forward knee drive (Figure 7-1, frames 9 through 12; Figure 7-2, frames 6 and 7). This combination of actions results in efficient arm and leg (thigh) movement and contributes to greater speed.

The arms play an important role in keeping the shoulders square to the direction of running, which in turn helps to keep the hips square so that the thighs move directly forward and backward. When hips turn sideways, the foot plant may show a zigzag pattern, which directs the Push-Off force somewhat to the side, rather than directly forward. In Figure 7-2, the hips remain square with the forward drive of the thighs.

For shoulders and hips to remain square (facing forward), the athlete must have strong abdominal obliques and lower-back muscles, which also maintain the appropriate upright position. The shoulders and neck should be relaxed even when striving to run faster and despite increasing fatigue. If these muscles tense, the resulting tightness across the neck and shoulders results in greater fatigue and restricted, ineffective arm movement.

Other Important Aspects of Technique

One important feature of running fast is the forceful forward drive of the thigh. The faster the thigh comes forward, the greater the stride length and the better the preparation for a forceful pawback movement. This in turn makes it possible to complete each stride more quickly, increasing stride frequency.

In sprinting, the knee is brought forward at maximum speed. When floor contact is made with the opposite leg, one thigh is visible from the side (Figure 7-1, frames 7 and 17). In other words, the forward-moving thigh lines up with the backward-moving thigh as full contact with the floor takes place. In some cases the swing leg is driven forward so forcefully it may be slightly in front of the support thigh. If it is slightly behind (Figure 7-2, frames 1 and 8), it indicates the need for a stronger, more powerful thigh drive.

For most players, especially when not in a fast break or full-sprint situation, the exact separation between the thighs at the moment of foot contact is not critical. The key element here is that the forward leg is in front of the body and moves backward prior to contact. This not only decreases the amount of braking forces, but also increases stride length and makes for faster, safer, more economical running.

To develop pawback action, reach forward with the foot when swinging the shin forward after the thigh is close to 60 to 70 degrees to the horizontal.

Frame 1   Frame 2   Frame 3   Frame 4

Frame 5   Frame 6   Frame 7   Frame 8

Figure 7-4

Do not lead with the foot in the forward thigh drive. The thigh must drive forward while the shin remains folded beneath the thigh. As the shin swings out, it more strongly prepares the hamstring muscles to then pull a near-straight leg down and back to contact the ground.

Hands and fingers should be relaxed at all times. The wrist should be relaxed and loose and held basically in a neutral position. In sprinting, it is possible to see the hand literally *flapping* during the run, indicative of high levels of relaxation. A fist or locked fingers indicates tension.

Head position governs body position and balance. Good posture includes the head directly above the shoulders, which should be directly above the hips, which are directly above the feet when in the Support phase. A forward lean of the head results in excessive forward lean overall and energy wasted to maintain balance (Figure 7-3). Leaning forward should only be used when accelerating.

A common sign of tension is facial strain. You should tell your athletes to smile every so often while running. When they feel a distinct change in their features, this indicates excessive tension. The more relaxed the non-running muscles are, the more effective running technique becomes, and the less the energy is used. By the way, this is not an absolute. If too relaxed, the athlete will not be able to run well. Some tension is needed for good posture and effective muscle action.

CHAPTER 8

Specialized Exercises for Running

The following exercises have been created from biomechanical and kinesiological analysis of world-class basketball players and runners. They have been used for many years and have proven both their safety and effectiveness. However, if you feel any major discomfort in executing these exercises, be sure to check on how you are doing the exercise, or if you have any physical problems that do not allow you to do them as needed and described. You must execute these exercises as described to get their full benefits and prevent injury.

This chapter is divided into two sections: *Strength Exercises* and *Explosive Exercises*. The two go hand-in-hand. The athlete must develop strength in order to maximize improvements in running technique. With this foundation in place, Explosive Exercises yield their most impressive results.

Strength Exercises

The following 15 exercises will help to develop the strength needed to maximize improvements in your running technique.

Heel Raises

Heel raises duplicate ankle-joint extension, the key action in the Push-Off. See Chapter 4 for a description of this exercise, which is illustrated in Figure 4-1.

Toe Raises

Toe raises duplicate the raising of the front part of the foot as occurs during the forward swing of the shin. They also help prevent shin splints. Toe raises balance calf-muscle development, allowing the athlete to develop even greater calf strength.

Execution with rubber tubing: Assume a seated position on the floor with the leg to be exercised extended and with one end of the rubber tubing attached to the ball of the foot area. The other end should be secured at the same height with tension on the cord. Point the toes as far as possible away from yourself, then pull the toe-ball area of the foot back toward the shin as far as possible (Figures 8-1a and 8-1b). Hold for one or two seconds in the up position. Repeat.

Figure 8-1a　　　　**Figure 8-1b**

Figure 8-1c

Figure 8-1d

Execution in the gym: Toe raises are done on a Tib Exerciser machine. Assume a seated position on an exercise bench and place the heels of the feet on the swivel-heel plate of the Tib Exerciser machine. The toe areas of the feet should be placed under the resistance rollers with the feet angled downward as much as possible (Figure 8-1c). When ready, raise the toe portions of the feet as high as possible (Figure 8-1d). Hold for one to two seconds, and then lower at a moderate speed. Repeat after reaching the initial position. (Note: The feet cannot be raised much above the horizontal position. Go through the maximal range of motion from the extended-ankle position.)

Standing Leg Curl

This exercise develops hamstring strength, stabilizing the knee and reducing lower-thigh hamstring injuries. It also corrects excessive inward or outward rotation of the feet. Refer to Chapter 4 for a description of the standing leg curl, which is illustrated in Figure 4-3.

The Squat

The squat strengthens the anterior thigh (quadriceps) muscles to prevent excessive up-and-down movements during the Support phase. See Chapter 4 for a description of this exercise, which is illustrated in Figure 4-4.

The Standing-Leg Extension

Although they strengthen the same muscle that the squat does, leg extensions are recommended to help develop a stronger whipping forward of the shin prior to pawback. See Figure 4-2 in Chapter 4 for an illustration of this exercise.

The Lunge

This exercise actively stretches hip flexors and strengthens the quadriceps. The lunge prepares athletes for cutting actions and getting low. It provides the flexibility and strength needed to take a long step when reaching for the ball and to lower the body for movement in various directions. It also strengthens the quadriceps for stopping actions. When done with the Active Cord hip belt, it improves the speed and power of your first step.

Execution: Assume a well-balanced standing position with the feet hip-width apart. Hold dumbbells in the hands or a barbell on the shoulders. When ready, inhale and hold your breath. Step forward with a very long stride, keeping the trunk in a vertical position. Upon landing, hold the vertical trunk position and slowly lower the upper body straight down. In the bottom position, there should be approximately 90 degrees of flexion in the forward leg, and most of the weight should be on it. The rear leg should remain straight, but relaxed. There will be muscle tension in the front leg and lower back, with a strong stretch of the hip flexors of the rear leg.

After reaching the lowermost position, shift the weight backward while strongly extending the forward leg and taking several short steps to return to the original position. Exhale and repeat the exercise, stepping out with the other leg (Figures 8-2a through 8-2c).

It's also effective to rise up on the forward leg after each lunge (a walking lunge). This action strengthens the hip-extensor muscles. With sufficient hip-joint flexibility, the knee of the rear leg should almost touch the floor in the bottom position, while the leg is kept straight.

The Forward-Knee Drive

This duplicates the action of driving the thigh forward during the Push-Off.

Execution: Attach one end of a piece of rubber tubing (as in the Active Cords Set) to a stationary object about knee high and the other end to the attached strap around the ankle. Stand far enough away from the attachment so that there is ample tension on the cord when the leg is behind the body. Stand erect and hold onto a stationary object to stabilize the upper body (Figure 8-3a).

Figure 8-2a

Figure 8-2b

Figure 8-3a

Figure 8-2c

Figure 8-3b

When ready, drive the thigh forward vigorously. At the same time, bend the knee so that the shin remains basically parallel to the floor during the forward drive. The thigh should stop when it is approximately 45 to 60 degrees forward (Figure 8-3b). Do not drive the thigh upward. Maintain an erect-body position during execution. For variety, extend the support leg and rise up on the balls of the feet.

Pawback (Leg Pull-Down)

This improves the thigh-pullback action that occurs in preparation for touchdown.

Execution: Attach one end of an Active Cord to a high (above the head) stationary object and the other end to the ankle strap of the leg to be exercised. Stand back from the point of attachment so that the cord is vertical or at an angle to the body when raising the slightly bent leg to a below-parallel position (Figure 8-4a). There should be tension on the cord.

Figure 8-4a

Figure 8-4b

When ready, straighten the leg and pull down and back fairly vigorously. Contact on the ground should be on the whole foot or the ball of the foot directly under the body (Figure 8-4b). The body should be in an erect, stable position during execution.

Glute-Ham Gastroc Raise

This is the only exercise that strengthens the hamstring muscles and their tendons at the hip and knee joints in sequence. This provides power for pawback action. Players who do this exercise will rarely, if ever, experience hamstring injuries. Proper execution (as described in Chapter 4) can be achieved only on the Yessis Back Machine, formerly known as a Glute-Ham Machine. See Figure 4-6.

The Back Raise (Back Extension)

This exercise safely strengthens the lower-back muscles. It's the best exercise for strengthening the erector-spinae muscle of the lower back through the full range of motion. Strong muscles enable the athlete to maintain an erect-trunk position while running and help to prevent lower-back injury. The back raise is most conveniently and safely done on a Yessis Back Machine, or on a high sturdy table with an assistant holding the athlete's legs down. See Chapter 4 for a complete description of the back raise, which is illustrated in Figure 4-7.

The Good Morning

This exercise stretches and strengthens the hamstrings and upper tendons and stabilizes the spine. Refer to Chapter 4 for a description of this exercise, which is illustrated in Figure 4-5.

Reverse-Hip Extension

This involves the same hip muscles as the *Good Morning*. Because of the great need for hamstring strength in basketball, it is included here.

Execution: Lie facedown over the rounded seat of the Yessis Back Machine, or off the end of a high sturdy table holding the sides for support. The lower abdomen and pelvis should be supported on the far side of the curved seat or be over the table. Grasp the rollers or back plate to hold your head and shoulders in place. The legs should hang at a 60-degree angle (Figure 8-5a).

Place an attachment board under the front supports of the machine to secure it. Attach both ends of the rubber tubing to the hook directly under the leg or legs to be exercised. Wrap the middle of the cord around one or both legs. It's most effective to work one leg at a time. There should be slight tension on the tubing when in the down position.

When ready, inhale and hold breath while raising one leg until it is in line with or slightly higher than the level of the back (Figure 8-5c). After reaching the uppermost position, exhale and return to the initial position. Relax for a moment, then repeat. Do the exercise with both legs. Keep the leg straight while pulling it upward against the cord resistance. This exercise may also be done with ankle weights (Figure 8-5b).

Figure 8-5a

Figure 8-5b

Figure 8-5c

Shoulder Rotation

This strengthens the abdominal-oblique muscles in a manner more specific to running. Do with rubber tubing or on a cable machine.

Execution: Stand facing away from the attachment of the cable (rubber tubing). Hold the other end in one hand, shoulder high, with the arm bent at 90 degrees. Rotate the shoulders back toward the cable attachment, keeping the hips and toes on both feet facing forward. This is the starting position (Figure 8-6a). Inhale and hold your breath, while holding the arm in position. Rotate the shoulders forward to a front-facing position and slightly beyond. Return to the initial position and repeat (Figure 8-6b).

Yessis Back Machine Sit-Ups

This advanced exercise strengthens the lower section of the abdominals through a full range of motion. These muscles work together with the hip flexors in driving the thigh forward. This exercise is especially important for maximum speed.

Execution: Adjust the Yessis Back Machine so that when you're seated, support will be on the backside of the upper thighs and lower buttocks. The feet should be placed between the rollers, with the legs fully extended. Inhale slightly more than usual, and hold your breath while lowering the trunk

Figure 8-6a

Figure 8-6b

back and down until it is slightly below thigh level (Figure 8-7a).

The legs should remain straight at all times, producing tension in the abdominal, hip, and thigh muscles. Using the hip and abdominal muscles, curl trunk up and return to upright position (Figure 8-7b). Exhale at the end of the up phase. Execute at a moderate rate of speed.

Resistive Breathing

This exercise strengthens the inspiratory and expiratory muscles. This delays the onset of fatigue, improves cardiovascular endurance, and increases Vo2 Max. The major muscles involved in inspiration are the diaphragm and intercostals. In expiration, the internal and external obliques and the transverse abdominis are involved. To most effectively strengthen the respiratory muscles, use a resistive breathing device, such as the Sports Breather.

Execution: Adjust the resistance for inhalation and exhalation to better match individual capabilities. To exercise the muscles forcefully, inhale against the resistance, and then exhale forcefully against resistance at a steady rhythm for up to one minute. Relax for a minute and repeat (Figures 8-8a and 8-8b).

Breathing can be modified to simulate different needs and conditions. To simulate sprinting, the

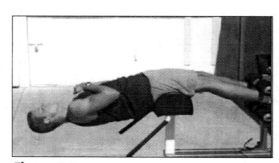

Figure 8-7a

Figure 8-7b

Figure 8-8a   **Figure 8-8b**

athlete can forcefully inhale, hold his breath, forcefully exhale, and so on. Because one of the key actions in breathing is forceful exhalation, concentrate on greater development of this ability. The faster and more forcefully an athlete can exhale, the quicker he can take in air for a more effective exchange of gases in the lungs. Strengthening the respiratory muscles is beneficial for players and athletes who have asthma.

Explosive Exercises

The explosive power seen in sprinting comes mainly from leg actions. To increase the ability of the leg muscles to contract explosively, it is necessary to do speed-strength exercises, i.e., exercises that combine speed with strength (such as plyometrics). This is the key to increasing explosive power and running speed.

Speed-strength, or explosive training, entails some form of jumping or receiving and repelling a force. Many of the explosive exercises used to improve running speed are also used to improve jump height.

Before going into the exercises used to develop explosive power, it is important to understand that how the athlete jumps during these exercises is critical to the benefit he receives. When doing easy jump activities – such as simple hopping and skipping – technique is not critical. As jumps become more powerful (higher and farther), takeoff and landing become extremely important in relation to athletic development and injury prevention.

The following 14 exercises will help to improve overall running speed.

Explosive Heel Raises

These are basically the same as heel raise strength exercises, except for the speed of execution.

Execution: Position the balls of the feet on the foot platform. Inhale slightly more than usual and hold your breath. Lower the heels at a moderate rate of speed. Upon feeling a strong stretch of the Achilles tendon, quickly reverse directions and rise up as high as possible. Hold the up position for one to two seconds. Exhale and repeat. Transition from the down movement to the up movement as fast as possible, as described in the heel raises section of Chapter 4 (Figure 4-1). (Note: The range of motion is slightly less than when doing the exercise slowly.)

Squat Jumps

Refer to Chapter 4 for a description of squat jumps, which are illustrated in Figure 4-10.

Split-Squat Jumps

Refer to Chapter 4 for a description of this exercise, which is illustrated in Figure 4-11.

Explosive-Knee Drive

This is done in basically the same manner as the knee drive exercise for strength. The only difference is faster initial speed of execution and greater tension on the tubing (or weights on the cable).

Execution: When ready, inhale and hold your breath. Start the drive of the thigh forward as quickly as possible. Do not drive the knee all the way up to the level position. The key is to have maximum tension when beginning the forward movement so that the movement stops with the leg just slightly in front of the body, as shown in Figure 8-3b.

Jump Out of a Squat

In addition to improving reaction times and jumping (as described in Chapter 4), this exercise can improve quickness when taking the first step in a cutting or reaching action. Refer to Figure 4-12.

Skip Jumps (Power Skips)

Execution: Begin by taking a few steps. Push off the ground with one leg while driving the opposite knee upward. When leaving the ground, the Push-Off leg

Frame 1

Frame 2

Frame 3

Frame 4

Frame 5

Frame 6

Frame 7

Frame 8

Frame 9

Frame 10

Figure 8-9

should be fully extended, and the swing-leg thigh should approach level. Upon landing on the swing leg, take a short skip, and then jump using the opposite leg for the knee drive. Distance and speed of forward movement are not important in this exercise. Concentrate on maximum vertical height and ankle extension (Figures 8-9).

Double-Leg Jumps in Place

This exercise develops the kind of explosive power an athlete needs around and under the basket.

Refer to Chapter 4 for a description of this exercise, which is illustrated in Figure 4-13.

Double-Leg Jumps for Height and Some Distance

This develops explosive-leg power directed upward and forward. It's also great in the warm-up prior to sprinting.

Execution: This exercise is the same as double-leg jumps in place, except on the takeoff, which is performed with the body inclined slightly forward. Land 12 to 18 inches in front of the takeoff spot (Figure 8-10).

Frame 1

Frame 2

Frame 3

Frame 4

Frame 5

Frame 6

Frame 7

Frame 8

Frame 9

Figure 8-10

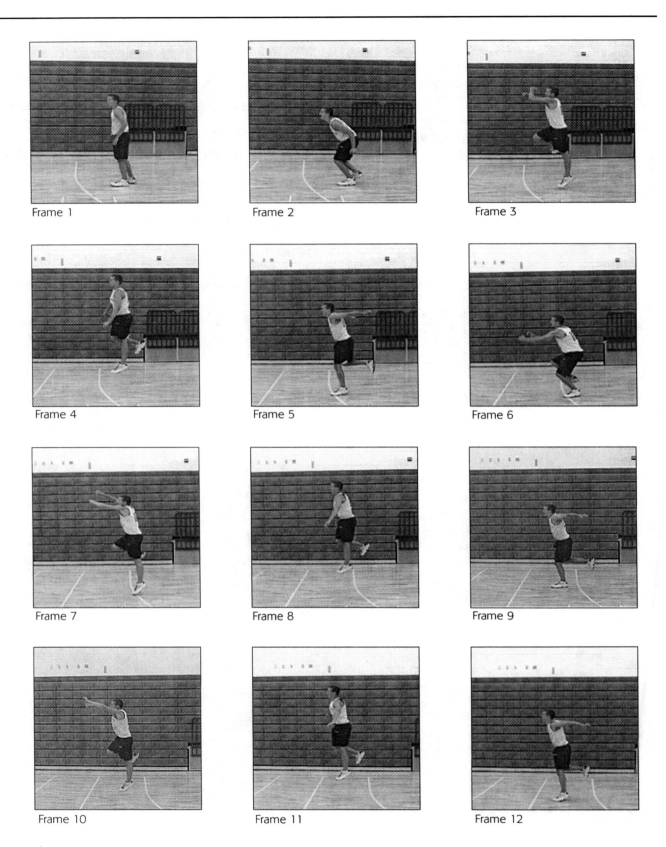

Frame 1

Frame 2

Frame 3

Frame 4

Frame 5

Frame 6

Frame 7

Frame 8

Frame 9

Frame 10

Frame 11

Frame 12

Figure 8-11

Single-Leg Jumps in Place

This exercise is more advanced than double-leg jumps and has greater specificity to running. Refer to Chapter 4 for a description of this exercise, which is illustrated in Figure 4-16.

Single Leg Jumps with Forward Movement

Execution: This exercise is the same as the single-leg jumps in place, but the forces are directed slightly forward on each jump. Land 12 to 18 inches in front of the initial takeoff point (Figure 8-11).

Ankle Jumps

Ankle jumps promote full range of motion when executing ankle-joint extension in the Push-Off. Refer to Chapter 4 for a description of ankle jumps, which are illustrated in Figure 4-17. It's recommended to do the explosive heel raise exercise before this exercise.

Frame 1

Frame 2

Frame 3

Frame 4

Frame 5

Frame 6

Frame 7

Frame 8

Frame 9

Figure 8-12

Frame 1

Frame 2

Frame 3

Frame 4

Frame 5

Frame 6

Frame 7

Frame 8

Frame 9

Frame 10

Frame 11

Frame 12

Frame 13

Figure 8-13

Double-Leg Jumps for Distance (Bounding)

Execution: Follow the instructions for the regular double leg takeoff for height, except for inclining the body forward at a 45-degree angle at takeoff. Extend the legs fully on takeoff. Upon landing, execute the next takeoff as quickly as possible. If sinking too low, or the jump is taking too long to execute, cut down on the distance (Figure 8-12). Jump for distance, not height.

Leaping

Leaping simulates the Push-Off and knee drive.

Execution: Take a few approach steps, then leap forward as far as possible taking off on one leg. The swing leg should be bent at the knee and driven forward at the same time as the Push-Off. The body should remain as low as possible in the takeoff and flight phases. Airborne position should be almost the same as in sprinting.

To prepare for landing, swing the forward leg down and back to push forward as forcefully as possible on the opposite leg. Be sure the trunk is erect and that the body is well in front of the push-off leg when ground contact is broken so that the forces are directed horizontally (Figure 8-13).

(Note: Do not confuse this exercise with what some coaches call single-leg bounding. In bounding, the takeoff is more vertical and the body does not remain low to the ground.)

Explosive Arm Drive with Tubing

This closely duplicates the arm action in sprinting.

Execution: Assume a standing position holding the handle of the active cord next to the body with the elbow raised and to the rear. When ready, inhale and hold your breath. Drive the arm forward while bending the arm to a 90-degree angle at the elbow. Drive the arm forward until the upper arm is next to the body and the hand is approximately shoulder high. Straighten the arm, return to the initial position under control, exhale, and prepare to repeat (Figures 8-14a and 8-14b).

Figure 8-14a

Figure 8-14b

The effects of many of these exercises, especially the knee drive, leaping, and jump exercises, can be increased by also using weighted shorts such as those by Protrain. Be careful using weighted shorts if the weights are positioned low on the thigh because they can cause stress on the hips.

CHAPTER 9

Quickness and Agility

While speed is an important physical asset, agility—the key to quickness—is even more important in basketball. Agility (or maneuverability) is the ability to change direction of the body, or its parts, as quickly as possible, whether in motion or from a stationary start.

The ability to make these changes (to move the body or arms and legs very quickly) is a major key to evading or keeping up with your opponent, stealing the ball, recovering loose balls, and blocking passes and shots. Considering all of these vital skills, the message is clear: agility is extremely important in basketball. The quicker and sharper your changes in direction (sharp 90-degree cuts), the more easily you can elude an opponent on offense or keep up with him on defense. As a result you become a better all-round player.

The Key Components of Agility

At its highest level, agility includes several traits: coordination, strength, explosiveness (speed-strength), reaction time, and speed of movement. These characteristics are exhibited in all forms of dodging, zigzag running, stopping and starting, moving in different directions quickly and sharply,

changing body positions, and moving the limbs into different positions quickly.

Improving each of these components leads to improved overall agility. For many players, agility is the key to their success, especially when they don't possess exceptional height or jumping abilities. One such player is Rob Dye (Bradley University, 1996-2000), who is pictured in this book. Using his extraordinary agility, Dye was among the best in all of college basketball at stealing the ball. However, after graduation he didn't make the Grand Rapids Hoop Team (CBA). The following season, after special training on his skills, especially speed and agility as outlined in this book, he made the team and the coaches were amazed at the differences in his performance. In 2002-2003, after even more improvement on his skills and physical abilities, he will play for the Gary Steelheads and is expected to be picked up by an NBA team.

Of all the physical qualities listed above, coordination is most important. It's a *must* for correctly executing the movements discussed in this chapter. Strength is also very important, especially eccentric strength. It's the key to stopping motion in one direction and creating the force needed to move in another. The eccentric contraction is also the key to speed-strength as it prepares the muscles for an explosive contraction. The greater an athlete's eccentric-contraction strength and ability to switch quickly from the eccentric to the concentric contraction, the more power (explosiveness) he'll be able to exhibit when executing various game skills.

Reaction time is important mainly when guarding an opponent. The best defenders anticipate and recognize an opponent's change in direction, and respond with quick, precise movements. Speed of movement and reaction time are intertwined. Of the two, speed of movement may be increased the most.

General Characteristics of a Cutting Action

To make a quick change in direction while in motion, the athlete must have adequate levels of strength (eccentric and concentric), speed-strength (explosive strength), flexibility (range of motion–ROM), and coordination (technique). Each of these components may be improved separately or in combination, enabling athletes to learn and improve movements quickly.

For example, before you can move in a different direction, it's necessary to stop your forward motion. The faster you are running, the more difficult this becomes, and the ability to make a sharp change in direction diminishes. However, the stronger you are, the faster you can go and still make a sharp change in direction. This is how improving your physical abilities can improve your performance greatly.

To stop forward motion, you must have sufficient eccentric strength. This is known as stopping strength. In essence, the muscles of the leg, especially the quadriceps, undergo a strong stretch and develop tension as the knee bends after planting the leg out in front to stop forward motion. Note that the initial landing takes place on the heel or on the inside border of the foot, followed by the whole foot as weight comes over the planted foot.

Frame 1

Frame 2

Frame 3

Frame 4

Frame 5

Frame 6

Frame 7

Frame 8

Figure 9-1

As the quadriceps lengthens, it develops greater tension. When the tension becomes sufficiently great, the knee bending and lower body motion stops. The upper body retains momentum; it can continue to move in an intended direction. This makes the cutting action more effective and enables the athlete to explode in a new direction.

Some of the actions described here seem obvious – so obvious that many athletes never think of them, much less analyze them in-depth. For instance, the quickest athletes probably never give a thought to planting the forward foot slightly to the opposite side of the intended cut, i.e., when cutting to the right, the athlete must plant his left leg out to the left (Figures 9-1, 9-2, 9-3, and 9-4). The plant may be slightly in front, depending on the direction and speed of approach.

A forward and left-side foot plant when moving forward essentially stops forward motion and creates an appropriate position for cutting to the right (Figure 9-4). Keep in mind that the cutting action can not be very sharp if made at high speed. Anticipation is important. To make a sharp 90-degree cut, slow down. For a 45- to 60-degree cut, forward motion can be faster (Figures 9-4 and 9-5).

Many coaches refer to the *athletic* position, and with good reason. Proper body position leads to greater agility. The lower the body, the more stable (resistant to movement) it is. This allows the body-position changes needed to cut. The taller (more erect) the body, the more difficult a change in direction becomes. When trying to make a one-step stop, the *tall* body tends to topple. Thus you should get low to stop and change direction but be tall when going into motion or when in motion.

To stop quickly, take a wide step out to the side or in front, then bend the stopping leg to lower the body, while keeping the trunk erect (Figure 9-3, frames 2 and 3; Figure 9-6, frames 3 and 4; Figure 9-7, frames 5 through 7; Figure 9-8, frames 3 and 4).

Frame 1   Frame 2   Frame 3   Frame 4

Frame 5   Frame 6   Frame 7   Frame 8

Figure 9-2

To elude a defender, look him in the eye when stepping out to the side and lowering your body. This reduces an opponent's ability to anticipate a change in direction. This does not preclude feinting actions (for example, a head fake).

Feinting actions are effective, but you should mix them up. For example, look an opponent in the eye with no movement of the head for one cut, then turn the head in one direction and cut to the other side on the next. There are many variants. The more you change how you execute feints, the more off-balance your opponent will be, increasing your effectiveness.

To execute the cutting action, when planting the leg to stop and lower the body, turn the hips together with the plant foot. The inside, non-cutting leg should be off the floor and free to move out (Figure 9-4, frames 3 and 4; Figure 9-5, frames 3 and 4; Figure 9-9, frame 3). Keeping the head and shoulders facing forward reduces the defender's ability to anticipate changes in direction.

Begin the Push-Off with the support leg in the new direction. At the same time, turn the hips and swing leg in the intended direction of movement. Step out with the non-support (free) leg in the new direction in preparation to move in that direction (Figure 9-2, frames 4 through 6; Figure 9-3, frames 2 through 5; Figure 9-4, frames 4 and 5; Figure 9-5, frames 4 and 5; Figure 9-6, frames 3 through 5; Figure 9-7, frames 6 through 8; Figure 9-9, frames 3 through 6; Figure 9-10, frames 4 through 6).

As weight shifts to the stopping (outside) leg, the other (inside) leg is unweighted and allowed to swing freely. When stepping out, the swing-leg foot hits the floor in the new direction of movement. The foot and most of the lower body should be fully turned, facing in the new direction. The rear foot breaks contact with the floor, ready to begin a new running stride (Figure 9-5, frames 3 through 5; Figure 9-6, frames 3 through 5; Figure 9-9, frames 5 through 7; Figure 9-10, frames 6 through 8; Figure 9-11, frames 3 through 5). (Note that most of the

Frame 1

Frame 2

Frame 3

Frame 4

Frame 5

Frame 6

Frame 7

Figure 9-3

athletes in these pictures have difficulty in turning only the lower body. This must be learned.) After one or more steps, the athlete should be able to cut in another direction, take a jump shot, or execute some other action.

Important Details of Cutting Actions

- Keep head and shoulders in place on the plant, and the opponent will not be able to read the next move (Figure 9-1, frames 4 and 5; Figure 9-2, frame 3; Figure 9-9, frames 1 through 4).

- Keep the trunk erect. Leaning over the stopping leg costs valuable time (Figures 9-1 through 9-12).

- The stopping leg should be out in front of the body (in relation to the new intended line of movement) with the upper body remaining in position (Figures 9-1 through 9-7, 9-9, 9-10, and 9-12).

- The plant leg should stop the body's forward motion and cushion some of the landing forces, while generating sufficient returnable force to push off in the opposite direction. The more powerful the eccentric contraction, which stops forward motion, the greater the accumulation of energy to prepare the muscles to contract explosively in the new direction (Figures 9-1 through 9-14).

All of these actions are accomplished in one step. That's right, one step! This is why this technique of executing a cut is so effective in increasing quickness and the ability to elude an opponent. All too often, athletes take two or three short *stutter* steps to stop their movement in one direction before stepping out into the new direction. This technique loses valuable seconds. Also, the defender knows a change in direction is coming and prepares himself to make a cut or movement of his own.

Frame 1

Frame 2

Frame 3

Frame 4

Frame 5

Frame 6

Frame 7

Figure 9-4

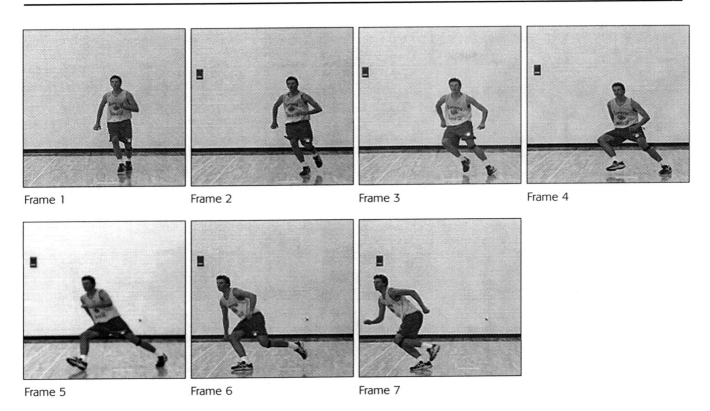

Frame 1 Frame 2 Frame 3 Frame 4

Frame 5 Frame 6 Frame 7

Figure 9-5

Frame 1 Frame 2 Frame 3 Frame 4

Frame 5 Frame 6 Frame 7

Figure 9-6

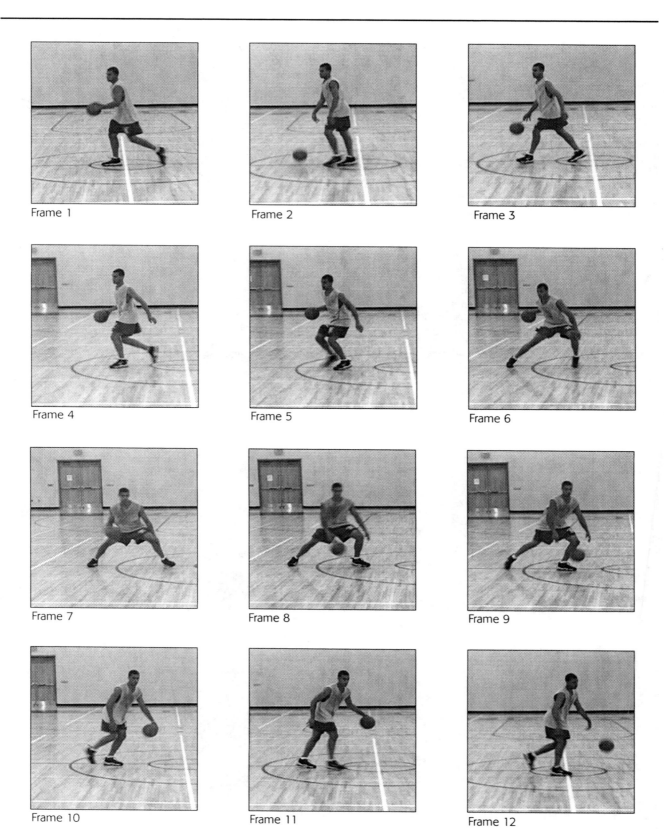

Frame 1

Frame 2

Frame 3

Frame 4

Frame 5

Frame 6

Frame 7

Frame 8

Frame 9

Frame 10

Frame 11

Frame 12

Figure 9-7

Specific Cutting Actions

The basic cutting technique is the same regardless of the specific cut to be executed. Consider the basic cuts: side-to-side, sharp (90-degree) cuts, angled (45-degree) cuts, forward-to-backward cuts, and backward-to-forward cuts. Each includes a stopping and lowering phase, and a sequential body turning action and a push-off, all executed in one step. Consider each of these cutting actions in detail.

Side-to-Side Cuts

Many athletes use a side-to-side *shuttle* step when moving laterally. This is effective when speed and quickness are not of major importance, and the athlete can adjust to opponents' movements before going into action. However, using a shuttle step to move laterally is very inefficient. It's recommended to use a cutting action similar to that described previously. Before beginning, run sideways as in a regular running stride while keeping the head and shoulders looking forward.

Execution:

- Plant the outside leg out to the side on the inner border of the foot to stop sideward motion (Figure 9-1, frame 3; Figure 9-2, frame 3; Figure 9-3, frame 2; Figure 9-7, frame 6).

- Drop the hips, but maintain a front-facing position with the head and shoulders. Bend the support leg in preparation for pushing off and raise the inside leg (Figure 9-1, frames 3 through 5; Figure 9-3, frames 2 through 4; Figure 9-9, frames 3 through 5; Figure 9-10, frames 3 through 5; Figure 9-12, frames 3 through 5).

- Push off with the stopping leg and step out with the inside-free leg in the new direction. Begin to turn the hips to the opposite side for movement in that direction. Combine this with the stepping out action (Figure 9-1, frames 5 and 6; Figure 9-2, frames 5 and 6; Figure 9-3, frames 4 and 5; Figure 9-12, frames 5 and 6).

- Turn the hips fully in the new direction while keeping the head and shoulders facing forward.

Frame 1

Frame 2

Frame 3

Frame 4

Frame 5

Frame 6

Frame 7

Frame 8

Figure 9-8

Frame 1 Frame 2 Frame 3 Frame 4

Frame 5 Frame 6 Frame 7

Figure 9-9

Frame 1 Frame 2 Frame 3 Frame 4

Frame 5 Frame 6 Frame 7 Frame 8

Figure 9-10

This enables the athlete to see the play and fool the opponent.

- Run in the sideward direction. Reverse directions again (if needed) without turning shoulders. Think of this as *swivel hips* (Figures 9-1 through 9-3, 9-9, 9-10, and 9-12).

- The cut to the right or left is executed in exactly the same manner (Compare Figures 9-1, 9-2, and 9-3 with Figures 9-9, 9-10, and 9-12).

There are many variations of this basic technique. The differences are not critical as long as the key elements are executed. For example, it's not uncommon to see some players actually leap before planting the stopping leg. As soon as the stopping leg hits, the other leg is free to step out in a new direction. When the support leg is planted, if the lower body is stationary and the swing leg is off the ground, it's still an effective method of executing the cut.

Many players turn the body late. They push off, and then turn as they go into the running stride. This too is acceptable and does not detract from speed of execution. Keep in mind that removing superfluous steps from the cut enhances quickness. If you simply stick the leg and push off in one motion, you will be faster than the person who must take two or more steps to execute the stop and then push off. Many players begin to stop on the inside leg first, stop on the outside leg, then execute the push and step out, or do a cross-over move with the legs. This slows the cutting action greatly.

Sharp (90-Degree) Cuts from Forward Movement

The ability to make a sharp, 90-degree cut is critical to getting open on the offensive end, and covering an opponent on the defensive end.

Execution:

- From a slow jog or walk, moving directly forward, plant the stride leg at a 90-degree angle to your path of movement opposite the direction in

Frame 1

Frame 2

Frame 3

Frame 4

Frame 5

Frame 6

Figure 9-11

which you wish to move. For example, for a cut to the right, while moving directly forward, plant the left leg out to the left, making contact on the inner side of the left foot (Figure 9-4, frames 4 and 5).

- On the plant, lower the body while keeping the upper body facing forward. Begin to turn the hips in the direction of the intended movement (to the right in this example). When the body is lowered and the weight moves on to the left (support) leg, lift the right (inside) leg (Figure 9-4, frame 4).

- Begin to push off with the left leg. Note that the stronger the eccentric contraction, the faster the stop, and the sooner the push-off. Turn the hips in the new direction of movement (Figure 9-4, frame 5).

- Conclude the push-off by fully extending the leg. Step out with the inside right leg, finish turning the upper body to the right, and take a short running stride with the body fully facing the new

direction of movement. Or keep the head and shoulders facing front while the hips and legs face the new direction (Figure 9-4, frame 6).

- Continue to accelerate or prepare to execute another action, or until another change in direction is called for.

Angled (45-Degree) Cuts

This cut is basically the same as the sharp cut to one side from a forward-moving direction. The main difference is that instead of making a sharp 90-degree cut to the right or left, the athlete makes a less-sharp, 45-degree cut while maintaining forward motion. This typically occurs at higher speeds, when blowing by a defender, or moving to an open spot for a pass. Speed and explosive cutting actions get the job done. Even a quick defender often falls a step or two behind. It helps to be close to your opponent when making the cut (Figures 9-5, 9-6, 9-8, and 9-11).

Frame 1

Frame 2

Frame 3

Frame 4

Frame 5

Frame 6

Frame 7

Frame 8

Figure 9-12

Execution:

- Plant the forward stride foot in front and out to the side, one to two feet to the side opposite your intended line of movement, i.e., at an angle of about 45 degrees forward and to the side (Figure 9-5, frames 3 and 4; Figure 9-6, frames 3 and 4; Figure 9-11, frames 3 and 4).

- Lower your body weight and begin to turn the hips in the new direction. The lower body's momentum stops, but the upper body continues to move forward and slightly to the side in reaction to the opposite-side foot plant.

    Pick up the inside leg in preparation for the push-off. Keep the head and shoulders facing forward so that the upper body appears to be moving forward (Figures 9-5, frame 3; Figure 9-6).

- Push off with the plant leg and move out at the desired angle (Figures 9-5, 9-6, and 9-8; Figure 9-11, frames 3 through 5).

- Turn the upper body away from your opponent. Stay close to him for evasive purposes. Step out in a forward-side direction with the inside leg. Resume the running stride (Figures 9-5, 9-6, and 9-8; Figure 9-11, frames 5 through 6).

- Execute all of these actions in one step.

Forward-to-Backward Cuts

This transitional type of movement occurs often in a basketball game. For example, Team A fast breaks, but loses the ball. Suddenly, attacking players become defenders. Figures 9-13 and 9-14 show the similarity between this and other cutting actions. Only the approach and change of direction are different.

Execution:

- Take a long forward step and turn the foot so the plant is on the inner side of the foot (Figure 9-13, frames 4 and 5).

Frame 1   Frame 2   Frame 3   Frame 4

Frame 5   Frame 6   Frame 7

Figure 9-13

- Keeping the head and shoulders in place, plant the leg and lower the body (Figure 9-13, frames 4 and 5). (Note: The pictured athlete does not have the needed flexibility to maintain shoulders in a forward-facing position.)

- Turn the hips and plant leg a full 90 degrees. This maximizes contact of the inside of the foot, providing a good stopping surface (Figure 9-13, frame 5).

- Though it appears as though the athlete is leaning backward, this is due to the lowered body position, forward plant of the leg, and holding the head and shoulders in place. Do not purposely lean to the rear, as it increases chances of slipping.

- Pick up the rear (non-stopping) leg, turn the hips toward the rear, and push off with the forward leg (Figure 9-13, frames 5 and 6).

Frame 1 Frame 2 Frame 3

Frame 4 Frame 5 Frame 6

Frame 7 Frame 8 Frame 9

Figure 9-14

- Push off and step out with the rear leg (now forward), turn the hips to the rear (new direction), and run to the rear (Figure 9-13, frames 5 and 7).

(Note: Athletes with sufficiently flexible midsections can look ahead, even while running backwards. Others must go backwards using a slower, back-pedaling action. The key point here is that it's possible to run *backwards* with the hips and legs in the new forward-running motion while the shoulders remain rotated to the rear. This allows all-important visual contact with the action. This form of running is much faster than running backwards with a back-pedaling action.)

Many coaches advocate back-pedaling to promote court vision and ball awareness. At times this positioning is needed, or even desirable. However, for speed, it's more effective to have the hips facing in the same direction as the run, while looking in the opposite direction. To do so, the athlete must be able to rotate the head and shoulders a full 90 degrees or more while the hips remain facing in the opposite direction. Such flexibility is critical for a basketball player, who must fall back quickly on defense while still looking at what the opponents are doing.

Backward-to-Forward Cuts

This is transition in reverse. Team A is sprinting back on defense when a turnover occurs. Instantly, the defending team goes on the attack. Players must stop their motion backward, turn their hips and legs to the front running position, and sprint in the opposite direction (Figure 9-14).

Execution:

- Plant the forward leg directly in front while simultaneously turning the hips 90 degrees to the side of the changing action. Keep the shoulders in place, or lean the head and shoulders forward slightly in the new direction (Figure 9-14, frames 5 and 6).
- Land on the ball and inside of the foot and then the whole foot while lowering the hips in one

long last stride to the rear (Figure 9-14, frames 4 through 6).

- Pick up the other leg so that it is free to step out.
- Step out with the free leg and push off with the rear leg forcefully. Turn the hips and shoulders to the full front-facing position. Move out as needed (Figure 9-14, frames 6 through 9).

Selecting the Cutting Leg

All cutting actions should be done on the outside leg. This means the leg planted opposite the direction of the cut. To cut right while moving forward, stop and push off with the left leg. To cut left, stop and push off with the right leg. When making a change in direction to go left while moving sideways to your right, stop and push off with the right leg. Push off with the left leg to go to the right.

When making a change in direction when moving forward or backward, stop and push off with whichever leg takes the last stride before the cutting action. If you stop and push off with the right leg, you should turn to your left. If you stop and push off with the left leg, you should turn to the right.

Do not push off with the leg on the same side as the intended direction, i.e. cut with the right leg to go right, or left leg to go left, except on rare occasions. This may happen when an opponent is blocking your pathway. In this case, cut on whichever leg is out in front. Understand, though, that this type of *same-leg* cutting action will not be as fast or sharp as the desired *opposite-leg* action. It requires the athlete to cross over his legs, resulting in awkward, non-athletic positioning. The reverse-side ankle action may also cause injury.

In spite of its ineffectiveness, many athletes still use this type of cutting action with the inside leg. It's strongly recommended that you check to see if you are one of these athletes, and then make the necessary changes. Always make the change in direction off the outside leg. The only times you should push off with the inside leg is when you are running a tight maze, or when you have to cut immediately on a signal or some action by your opponent. Such instances should be rare, however.

When you push off with the opposite leg, you'll get away from your defender more quickly, and as a result, be open. At the other end of the floor, you'll be able to keep up with your opponent when he makes quick changes in direction. These skills are particularly important for guards, whose effectiveness often hinges on the ability to execute quick changes of direction. The key to agility is to learn how to execute cuts and to improve physical abilities related to these movements with specialized strength and explosive exercises.

CHAPTER 10

Specialized Exercises for Agility and Cutting Actions

It's important to re-emphasize the relationship between *Strength Exercises* and *Explosive Exercises*. By increasing both strength and speed-strength (explosiveness), athletes position themselves to gain maximum benefit from the techniques described in Chapters 7 and 9. Improved technique is much easier to achieve with a foundation of strength in place.

Strength Exercises

All cutting actions involve some of the same leg and hip actions used in running. Some of the exercises for improvement of running also enhance cutting ability. The following are 13 strength exercises selected and described with agility, quickness, and cutting techniques in mind.

Leg Abduction

Leg (hip) abduction is the main action in stepping out to the side to plant the stopping leg, as well as the key action to initiate the push off when driving the hips (body) in the new side direction. The action in this exercise occurs in the hip joint. The exercise is called leg abduction because the leg is in motion, not the hips.

Execution with rubber tubing: Stand with one end of the rubber tubing attached to an ankle strap around the leg to be in motion and the other end to a stationary object. Stand sideways with the leg to be exercised farthest from the attachment so that the cord goes across the body. When ready, assume a well-balanced standing position, holding on to a workout partner for support and to maintain the upper body in place at all times. Inhale and hold your breath. Pull the leg out to the side as far as possible. Do not lean toward your partner. After reaching the uppermost position, exhale and return to the initial position. Pause and repeat. When pulling the leg out to the side, keep the toes pointed directly in front. Execution should be fairly vigorous in order to reach as high a position as possible while still keeping the upper body in place (Figure 10-1).

Hip Abduction

To duplicate even more closely the action of driving the hips forward when pushing off, do the hip abduction exercise with the hips in motion rather than the leg. Use Active Cords or a pulley cable machine with the non-slip belt.

Execution in the gym and with Active Cords: Secure the non-slip belt around the hips with one

Figure 10-1a

Figure 10-2a

Figure 10-1b

Figure 10-2b

end of the rubber tubing attached to the side of the hip and the other to an immovable object. When ready, keep the feet and shoulders in place and drive the hips sideways. Upon mastering this action, pick up the non-support (front) leg and step out while driving the hips (entire upper body) forward with a strong push off the rear leg. This gives the feel of the push off and driving the hips at the same time (Figures 10-2a and 10-2b).

Hip Adduction

Although hip-joint adduction is not a key movement in cutting, except when you cut off the inside leg, the adductor muscles must be strong to balance the abductor muscles, as well as to prevent groin injury when executing a cutting action and stepping out. Strength of the adductors is also important in pulling the outside leg in when going into the side-

running pattern and to bring the leg toward the midsection of the body when executing different evasive movements. This is best done with rubber tubing or on a low pulley cable machine.

Execution in the gym or with rubber tubing: Stand with feet apart with the inner leg to be exercised attached to the rubber tubing at the ankle. The other end of the tubing should be attached to an immovable object close to the ground. When ready, shift your weight to the outside leg (toward your partner). Keeping the leg to be exercised straight, pull it in to the other leg. Return to the initial position and repeat. Inhale and hold your breath when pulling the leg in. Exhale when returning to the initial position. Keep the upper body erect so that there is no leaning during the pull. Also hold on to a partner to maintain an erect, stable position (Figures 10-3a and 10-3b).

Figure 10-3a

Figure 10-4a

Figure 10-3b

Figure 10-4b

The Lunge

The lunge promotes the flexibility and strength needed to take a long step when reaching for the ball and to get the body low when moving in various directions. It's also important for strengthening the quadriceps for stopping actions and for stretching the hip flexors. Refer to Chapter 8 for an explanation of the lunge, which is illustrated in Figure 8-2. The lunge is also effectively executed with Active Cords and using the non-slip hip belt for more quickness on the first step.

Side Lunge

The side lunge is critical for cutting sideways and in taking a long sideward step. This exercise promotes flexibility of the hip-joint adductor muscles, which are often injured in side movements, and develops maximum range of motion and the ability to lower

the body as needed when taking a long step out to the side.

Execution in the gym: Assume a comfortable standing position with the feet approximately hip width apart. Hold a barbell on the shoulders with the arms extended and holding the bar. When ready, step out directly to the side and plant the foot at a 45-degree angle. Keep the trunk erect. Once the foot is firmly on the ground, lower the body directly downward until there is approximately a 90-degree angle in the lunging leg. The rear push-off leg should remain straight, resulting in a strong stretch on the inner thigh. Hold for one to two seconds, and then push off the forward foot to bring the weight backward. Rise up and repeat (Figures 10-4a and 10-4b). Exercise may be done one leg at a time, or in an alternating manner. The exercise can also be done with Active Cords, using the hip belt for increased speed in the first step out to the side.

Reverse Sit-Up

The reverse sit-up strengthens the lower abdominals, which play an important role in driving the swing-leg thigh forward in running, and forward and up when taking the first step in a cutting action push-off and in running.

Execution in the gym: Start flat on your back, with the arms alongside the body and feet off the floor, knees bent and thighs vertical (Figure 10-5a). When ready, inhale slightly more than usual and hold your breath. Rotate the pelvis up and toward the shoulders until hips are off the floor (Figure 10-5b). Keep knees bent tightly, isolating the action to the lower abdominals.

Push down with the hands to help raise hips (and legs) and ensure adequate rotation of the pelvic girdle. In the ending position, knees should be chest-high. Keep head and shoulders relaxed throughout the upward movement. Exhale as returning to the initial position, pause, and repeat.

When this exercise becomes easy, place the arms overhead so that they cannot assist in execution. Do the exercise using only the lower abdominals to rotate the hips upward. To involve more of the upper portion of the abdominal muscles, continue rotating the pelvis and legs up and over until the knees are close to the head. This is a more advanced movement. It provides more dynamic stretching of the lower back (Figure 10-5c).

Reverse-Trunk Twist

The reverse-trunk twist effectively develops midsection flexibility and strength of the abdominal-oblique muscles. The athlete who can do the reverse-trunk twist with fairly straight legs has the ability to turn the hips and legs in one direction while the upper body is rotated a full 90 degrees or more in an opposite direction. This is extremely important in all forms of cutting. It's also a great backstretch and helps keep the shoulders from rotating when running.

Execution in the gym: Lie face-up on the floor with arms out to the sides and palms down. Arms should be perpendicular to the trunk so that the body forms a letter T. Raise legs (thighs) to a 90-degree angle to the floor (Figure 10-6a). Then lower the legs to one side while continuing to hold the 90-degree angle in the hip joints. Touch the floor with the outside of the lower foot if the legs are relatively straight (more difficult), or with the outer knee if the legs are bent. Keep the shoulders and arms in full contact with the floor at all times

Figure 10-5a

Figure 10-5b

Figure 10-5c

(Figure 10-6b). Inhale and hold your breath while raising the legs back up to the initial position, and without stopping, over to the opposite side until touching the floor again (Figure 10-6c). Exhale while lowering the legs, then inhale and hold your breath while raising the legs. Alternate sides on each repetition.

Figure 10-6a

Figure 10-6b

Figure 10-6c

Hip Rotation

The ability to rotate the hips in one direction while facing in another direction is a key element in all cutting actions. Players who can easily rotate the hips are said to have *swivel hips* — the key to faking out an opponent. One of the simplest hip-rotation exercises is done with rubber tubing, such as the Active Cords set mentioned in Chapter 1.

Execution with Active Cords: Attach the non-slip belt around the hips and secure it firmly. Attach one end of the rubber tubing to the ring in front of the right hip, or right on the right hip, and stand with the right side in line with the attachment of the other end of the tubing at approximately hip height (Figure 10-7a). When ready, shift your weight onto the right leg (slide hips forward) to create more tension in the tubing. Turn (rotate) the hips to the right against the resistance of the tubing (Figure 10-7b). To develop the muscles needed in rotating the hips to the left, execute in the opposite manner, i.e., attach the rubber tubing to the right hip and stand with left side to the stationary attachment.

Figure 10-7a

Figure 10-7b

The Squat

The squat is an important exercise to develop not only the eccentric strength needed for stopping, but also the concentric strength for pushing off. Both are needed for explosive power. Refer to Chapter 4 for a description of this exercise, which is illustrated in Figures 4-4a through 4-4e. Consider doing a variant known as the delay squat (also described in Chapter 4).

Heel (Calf) Raises

Ankle-joint extension is an important action at the end of the push-off. It gives greater power on the takeoff in cutting and running. Refer to Chapter 4 for a description of this exercise, which is illustrated in Figures 4-1a through 4-1d.

Ankle-Joint Abduction

This exercise strengthens the muscles that are typically involved in ankle sprains. Note that ankle taping limits the joint's range of motion. Interestingly enough, studies show that within 15 minutes of beginning play, the tape stretches and no longer provides strong support. Strengthening the muscles surrounding the ankle reduces injury and enhances cutting actions. Do not rely on tape; it is a crutch that limits performance.

Execution with rubber tubing: Assume a seated position with the leg straight and one end of the rubber tubing attached to the inner side of the ball of the foot or mid-foot area. The other end should be attached low to the floor, with tension on the tubing in the beginning position (Figure 10-8a). When ready, turn the sole of the foot to the inside as far as possible while keeping the foot square to the shin. There should still be ample tension on the tubing. After reaching the farthest position, turn the sole of the foot outward as far as possible. Do not rotate the shin to point the toes in or out (Figure 10-8b). Repeat at moderate speed.

Ankle-Joint Adduction

This is the opposite action of ankle abduction. It also helps prevent ankle sprains when the sole of the

Figure 10-8a   **Figure 10-8b**

foot is turned outward. To execute, sit with the rubber tubing attached to the outside of the foot. Execution is the same as in ankle abduction except that the sole of the foot turns inward against the resistance of the tubing (Figures 10-9a and 10-9b).

The Forward-Knee Drive

This exercise enhances the all-important *first step* you hear so many coaches talk about. It helps improve the ability to accelerate. Refer to Chapter 8 for a description of the forward knee drive, which is illustrated in Figure 8-3.

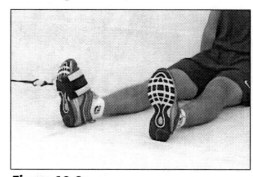

Figure 10-9a

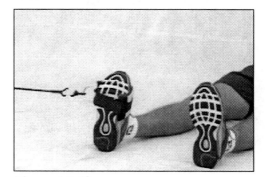

Figure 10-9b

Explosive Exercises

Many of the explosive exercises described for use in running are also effective in improving cutting actions. Remember, this is based on the athlete's ability to execute effective cutting actions. With poor technique, explosive exercises have minimal value.

In addition to the previously described exercises, there are still other exercises and drills that improve cutting ability. For example, when the push-off takes place in cutting action, the hips are turning in the direction of the run. The leg is often in a side-facing position to the hips when the actual push-off occurs. Double-leg and single-leg side jumps duplicate this action.

Double-Leg Side Jumps

Execution in the gym: Stand with both feet together in an erect, well-balanced position. When ready, bend the knees and leap up and out to one side while keeping the head and shoulders in place. Only the hips and legs should move out to the side. Upon landing, cushion and then jump back to the other side. Again, cushion the landing, withstand the landing forces, and immediately jump in the opposite direction keeping both legs together.

The key is to jump as far as possible sideways while still executing the change in direction as quickly as possible. Leaping too far to the side may result in sinking too low on the landing. Cut down the distance until achieving the right combination of distance and quickness. Alternate jumps to the left and right for up to 10 repetitions (Figure 10-10).

Single-Leg Side Jumps

Single-leg side jumps may be the most important exercise an athlete can do to enhance cutting actions. They duplicate exactly what occurs when cutting with the outside leg.

Frame 1   Frame 2   Frame 3   Frame 4

Frame 5   Frame 6   Frame 7   Frame 8

Figure 10-10

Execution in the gym: Stand with your weight equally balanced between both legs, spaced about hip- or shoulder-width apart. When ready, put all of the weight on one leg, and bend it slightly. Forcefully extend the leg and raise the other leg while leaping out to the side. Land on the outside (free) leg, and as soon as the foot touches down, cushion and withstand the landing forces, and immediately push off in the opposite direction to land on the opposite leg. Jump from the left leg to the right leg and from the right to left in an alternating manner (Figure 10-11).

(Note: When doing double-leg or single-leg side jumps, do not use hurdles. The idea is to promote quick sideward (as opposed to upward) movement. All sideward jumps should be done low to the ground, without any leaping up and down. Also, hurdles can cause injury when an athlete contacts or lands on them.)

When doing side jumps, do not use angled boxes or slopes, as on some slide boards. Using a side-angled surface promotes the opposite ankle-

Frame 1 Frame 2 Frame 3

Frame 4 Frame 5 Frame 6

Frame 7 Frame 8 Frame 9

Figure 10-11

joint action from what actually occurs in a true-cutting action when the outside-leg foot is planted on the ground. It's much more safe and effective to do strengthening exercises for the ankle on a flat surface, such as a basketball court. This allows for the full range of ankle-joint action, which is often very great, as opposed to the restricted motion promoted by angled boxes.

Jump Out of a Squat on One Leg

Assume a half-squat position on one leg and hold for two to four seconds in preparation for leaping (jumping out). When ready, jump to the opposite side of the leg being used as powerfully as possible, i.e., if standing on the right leg, leap to the left (Figure 10-12, frames 1-4). Do on both legs. The direction of the jump can be changed on each jump.

Explosive Drills

Four-Way Cuts

Having mastered the ability to cut backward, sideward, and forward, athletes can do the four-way cut drill individually or in groups. To execute, assume a ready position (the athletic stance) and face the coach leading the drill. The coach gives a verbal or hand signal indicating the direction in which the

athletes must move (cut) and then take one or two quick running steps. He then changes the direction, requiring a quick cut or change in direction. There is no set pattern in this drill. Learn to execute a cut in any and all directions while in movement in any direction (Figure 10-13). Execute for up to 30 seconds (or slightly more), but always stop before fatigue sets in and athletes are cutting in opposite directions. Inability to execute this drill indicates the need for more individual work and concentration on specific cuts.

The Two-Man Approach and Cut

This drill simulates offensive and defensive cutting situations. To do the drill, two athletes should stand about five yards away from a *centerline* (10 yards apart) facing each other. When ready, both walk or jog toward the centerline where the person who's designated as being on offense makes a sharp cut in either direction. The partner must react and move quickly to keep up. Note that in Figure 10-14 the players are not close to one another. This was done to illustrate the movement pattern clearly.

Master this drill first from (in order) a walk, a jog, and a slow run. At first, execute a sharp, 90-degree cut. Do not travel forward when making the cut. When running at faster speeds, execute a 45- to 60-degree cut. This is especially important for guards.

| Frame 1 | Frame 2 | Frame 3 | Frame 4 |

Figure 10-12

Frame 1   Frame 2   Frame 3

Frame 4   Frame 5   Frame 6

Frame 7   Frame 8   Frame 9

Frame 10

Figure 10-13

Frame 1

Frame 2

Frame 3

Frame 4

Frame 5

Figure 10-14

CHAPTER 11

Designing a Personalized Training Program

Elite-level athletes understand that weight (strength) training leads to greater speed, power, and overall performance. Surprisingly, many basketball players and coaches still believe that weight training makes them slower, less flexible, and more injury-prone. Ignore the myths. Properly designed and executed weight training is a basketball player's ally.

Through weight training, an athlete can: improve his shooting technique, increase his running speed and quickness, increase his muscular and aerobic endurance, prevent injury, and increase his jump height. For the purpose of this book, the focus will be on speed and quickness.

By designing and tailoring a weight-training program to address individual needs, it's possible to develop virtually any specific type of strength. This includes strength-endurance, absolute and relative strength, speed-strength, eccentric strength, explosive strength, and starting strength. Don't think of strength training simply as a means of getting bigger or stronger. Think of it as a means of improving specific aspects of your play.

Before setting up a weight-training program, consider factors that may influence the overall process. A good example is time. Many coaches and

athletes cite the time factor as a major objection against a separate strength development program. As a result, they integrate strength training with basketball drills (for example, running up hills and/or stairs).

While these programs are somewhat effective, they don't meet the goals of special strength training. Why? Simply because basketball drills and stair running lack a key element: progressive overload. The athlete and/or trainer cannot regulate the intensity of the loads, requiring the muscle to respond with continual increases in strength. Running stairs, which is not even specific to basketball and can teach bad habits, does not lead to increased strength (except when first starting).

As important as strength increases are, the main objective is to play better, not to be the strongest player on the team. Time is a precious commodity. Why spend it on non-productive training? Use it to develop the kind of strength needed to enhance specific skills and play the game better.

Because specific strength is developed through specific adaptation to the demands placed on the muscle, overloading must be carried out in a progressive manner. Pulley weights, rubber tubing, and/or free weight training (dumbbells and barbells) are the proper equipment for developing the kinds of strength basketball players need. They require comparatively little total energy output, weather conditions do not prohibit their use, and resistance may be adjusted to match an individual athlete's needs and abilities.

> Additional advantages of weight (resistance) training with adjustable weights and rubber tubing:
>
> - Gradual increases in resistance promote the progressive overload described previously. This assures a continuity of strength gains in the desired actions or body areas.
>
> - Resistance training develops strength in any or all of the body's muscles, meeting the specific demands of the game. For example, the thigh-drive exercise, which develops the hip-flexor strength needed for an explosive first step, is done most effectively with rubber tubing or on a pulley cable.
>
> - You can design and tailor a strength-development program focused on those muscles that facilitate effective use of the speed, skill, endurance, and tactics competitive basketball requires.

The key is individualization, i.e., personalizing your training program. By this, I mean any number of things. Are you a recreational or competitive player? What position do you play? Have you mastered the exercises and game skills described earlier in this book? Remember, as your level of fitness improves, you can (and should) increase the difficulty of your weight-training regimen.

Getting Started

For beginners (and those who have not worked out for extended periods), a learning and familiarization stage is necessary. This accustoms the body to exercise gradually, without soreness or discomfort. To begin, read (and sometimes re-read) exactly how to do the exercises. Have this book with you when you train, or when training an athlete.

Learning, Modifying, and Perfecting Game Skills

To make *technique work* most effective, follow these guidelines:

- Always be in an energetic and alert state of mind. All skills are neuromuscular skills. They require active involvement of the nervous system and the muscular system. The nerves and muscles must be energetic to carry out specific movements with the necessary precision. Do technique work first (or separately) when physically and mentally fresh.

- Do not repeat one action for an excessively long period of time. Always stop at the first signs of fatigue or when losing the desired precision. A fatigued athlete develops a different neuromuscular pathway for execution of the skill. This is not desirable. Learn the technique one way, and reinforce it in the same way until it becomes automatic. The body will then make the necessary changes when in a fatigue state to ensure effective execution of the skill.

- Keep practice periods relatively short. When working on cutting or running technique, it's important to concentrate on the movements being executed. After 10 to 20 repetitions, switch to a different skill or element.

- Follow the technique work with specialized strength exercises to reinforce the exact movements seen in various joint actions. For example, when working on the knee drive to improve quickness or running speed, do the knee-drive exercise. This reinforces the feel of driving the knee forward. This enhances the technique execution. This special strength work takes maximum concentration to develop the correct pathway and the muscle feel needed to duplicate the skill in game play.

Learning, Modifying, and Perfecting Physical Abilities

Do one exercise for three to five repetitions with light resistance. When using rubber tubing, adjust the length to execute the exercise easily through a full range of motion. This means doing the exercise (up and down or away and back) three to four times. Execute each repetition at a moderate rate of speed.

Concentration, precision, and feel are important. They help the athlete recognize how an exercise relates to specific basketball skills. After completing three to five repetitions, relax, and prepare for the next exercise. Read the description and do several repetitions. Proceed in this manner until completing the selected exercises.

When beginning, select exercises that address *trouble* areas or those joint actions in need of improvement. Add exercises in a week or so, supplementing the core group originally selected.

A sample strength-exercise program may include the following 10 exercises: good morning, back raise, knee drive, heel raise, squat, triceps push-down, reverse-trunk twist, reverse sit-up, biceps curl, and lateral-arm raise. For many athletes, this sample program is sufficient for the first two to six weeks, especially in regard to learning the exercises. Keep an accurate record of the number of repetitions performed during each workout.

Personalize a Training Program

Never copy what someone else is doing. Each athlete responds differently to exercise programs. Each has his own rate and amount of potential development. Copying someone else's program increases the risk of injury.

When to Work Out

Schedule workouts so that they are not immediately before or after play. An ideal situation is to exercise in the morning and play (or practice) in the afternoon. The reverse is certainly acceptable. The key is rest and recovery between activities. Consistent scheduling provides ample time for recovery and adaptation to the exercises.

Reps and Sets

When beginning, do one set of each exercise. The term set means doing a particular number of repetitions of one exercise one time. For example, 20 repetitions maximum (RM) of the squat constitutes a set. An additional 20 (or fewer) RM constitutes set number two.

Add one to two repetitions at each workout (or each week) until reaching a 15 to 20 RM. Don't exceed this number. When repeatedly reaching 20 RM or more, increase the resistance for that particular exercise.

Once an athlete's comfort and confidence increase, he may want to add exercises to the program. Soreness on the day of or immediately after a workout suggests too many repetitions and/or too much resistance. When this happens, use the same (or less) resistance in the next workout. Upon recovery, gradually increase resistance or repetitions.

Remember, the main purpose of the workout program at this time is to familiarize the athlete with the exercises, allowing his body to adapt to the workout. Doing more than one set does not produce greater or faster results. Additional sets play their most important role only after an athlete achieves a level of comfort, fitness, familiarity, and precision.

Days Per Week

Work out three days per week. Workouts should last 30 to 60 minutes. The athlete gains sufficient strength and flexibility to run and cut faster with a maximum of 90 to 180 minutes of working out per week. This is especially true of players who have never strength trained. Higher-level players may require more time because of their need for specific strength and speed-strength training.

Work out on a regular basis. When on a *3-days-a-week program*, don't skip days and say, "I will do four days next week because I only did two this week." This is not effective. Working out more than three days per week does not bring additional benefits. Conversely, it may lead to overtraining, injury, and soreness. A 3-days-a-week program allows muscles ample recovery time. As a result, it will not interfere with actual practice or play. Once a certain fitness level is achieved, working out four to six times per week may be successfully integrated with playing.

Continuing to play is important. It allows the athlete opportunities to incorporate minor adjustments and newly learned skills into his game. Most of these changes will occur subconsciously. The changes will feel very natural. You shouldn't do all-out sprints or cuts at this time. Not only may this lead to injury, it reduces concentration on form and technique changes.

Increasing the Difficulty

Upon reaching 15 to 20 RM for each exercise (when the exercises become easy), the athlete may be ready to make changes. At this time, workouts become more strenuous. When an athlete reaches 20 RM regularly, he should increase the resistance. The increased resistance results in decreased repetitions—perhaps 12 to 15 RM. Gradually work back up to 20 RM and repeat the process.

Regardless of resistance, the last repetition of any given set should be the most an athlete can do with proper technique. Do not, for example, do 15 or 20 repetitions and still feel refreshed. The athlete should feel slightly out of breath and have muscular fatigue at the end of a set.

Making the Workout More Specific

Gear workouts toward those qualities to be improved, keeping in mind that each position and level of play demands something different from the athlete. Recreational play differs from competitive play. A center needs one set of skills; a guard a completely different set.

Beginners may achieve great improvement from doing only one or two sets of 15 to 20 RM. At this time, pure strength is not be as important as raising levels of muscular and cardiovascular endurance. A more advanced player needs greater levels of strength (both eccentric and concentric) as well as greater levels of speed-strength, starting strength, and explosive strength. Programs for beginners and advanced players must be different, even if they include some of the same exercises.

Developing Strength

To increase strength after basic training, do two to four sets of key specific exercises. Using greater resistance (which is needed for greater strength) requires warm-up or initial preparation of the muscles. For the first set (when doing three or more sets), do 10 repetitions at half the resistance of set two. In set two, do 8 to 10 RM for strength. For even greater strength, add a third set of 8 to 10 RM. Add a set of 15 to 20 RM for muscular endurance. Completing three to four sets (a warm-up set, one to two sets for strength, and a set for endurance) is sufficient for most players.

After doing the first set, rest 30 to 60 seconds. Repeat the same exercise for the second set. To do more exercises in less time, add an exercise for different muscles between sets. At high intensity levels, consider a split program; do upper and lower body exercises twice a week on alternate days with two days of rest for each. For example, Monday and Thursday: upper body. Tuesday and Friday: lower body. Wednesday and Saturday: special workouts for other qualities, such as flexibility, agility, coordination, etc. You shouldn't use too much resistance, which may decrease Range of Motion (ROM) and negatively affect an athlete's play.

Speed-Strength and Explosive Training

Strength coupled with speed is important for more advanced players who need this type of training to increase speed and quickness. This is not for beginners. For the most part, only those with a well-established strength base should do speed-strength and explosive training.

Some forms of explosive training, such as introductory plyometrics, can be done without a high-level strength base. The explosive work is not intense and consists mainly of easy jump exercises that are usually safe. If you do strength training three times a week, introductory speed-strength work is done on the alternate days but no more than two to three times a week.

The introduction of explosive and speed-strength work should be slow and gradual. Begin with easy preparatory-type jump exercises, as well as combinations of strength and explosive movements. A good example of the latter is holding a squat position with resistance for four to five seconds, and then exploding upwards. To ensure a slow and gradual introduction to this kind of training, begin with simple skipping, hopping, jumping, leaping, and bounding. These activities prepare the muscles for more intense work later.

If following a four-day split program, consider sequencing speed-strength work and strength training. Do the speed-strength work first (after a vigorous warm-up). Follow up with strength and (if desired) endurance work. Build intensity levels gradually over a period of four to eight weeks.

Athletes who are capable of doing high intensity jumps correctly are ready for a maximum intensity workout. Gradually increase the number of exercises that are done explosively. Begin with a few exercises, and then increase the number of exercises and/or sets for each exercise. Do each exercise correctly to get maximum benefits and prevent injury.

Beginners and young players (ages 6 to 12) should use speed-strength and explosive training sparingly. Initially, aerobic capabilities and strength are most important, and up to 90% of training should be devoted to these areas. Speed work should comprise about 10% to 20% of workouts. Beginners should do only three to four speed-strength or lead-up plyometric exercises for one to two sets in the training session. These exercises should precede strength and/or endurance training.

The intensity of an advanced athlete's work when doing speed-strength and explosive training is very high. More rest is needed between sets, making workouts longer than usual. Do this type of training only in the specialized period of training (after general conditioning and before competition). Because this type of training has a strong residual effect, stop such training at least one to two weeks before major competition. This gives muscles ample time to adapt and be ready for all-out performance during competition.

Speed Training

Speed and quickness training consists mainly of all-out sprints, explosive strength exercises, and agility (cutting) exercises. You should do these no more than two times a week (except when learning technique).

Especially important at this time are specialized exercises that duplicate what occurs in the hip joints, the source of most of your speed and quickness in running and cutting. Practical experiences have shown that developing the muscles as they are used in running and cutting improves speed and quickness significantly and without any additional running. When specialized explosive exercises and speed are both practiced, the results are even more impressive.

In sprinting, it's important to maintain good running technique. When fatigue sets in, technique changes as the athlete develops different neuromuscular pathways. However, when the nervous system is fresh, the athlete can duplicate exactly the correct technique, ensuring the fastest (and safest) running and cutting. For this reason, speed and quickness training should always precede other types of training.

The same holds true for explosive work. Allow ample rest between exercises or sets so that the muscles are always capable of a maximal contraction when doing the most intense forms of explosive training. Explosive exercises should never be done in a fatigue state.

When changing or modifying running or cutting technique, avoid all-out speed training. Master the desired technique, and then gradually increase speed and quickness while maintaining good technique. A gradual approach precludes relapses to old, ineffective techniques.

All-out speed training and heavy weight training are not compatible. Decrease high-intensity strength training and increase speed-strength training when introducing all-out speed training. Speed work is most effective after completing the strength-training phase and in conjunction with the specialized explosive exercises.

Overspeed training—encouraging the body to move faster than it would volitionally—can be effective at this time. Such training is important for teaching the nervous system what it is like to act faster and quicker. There are various ways of achieving overload (running downhill, with a parachute or with weighted shorts), but the application of each method must be precise. For example, when using weighted shorts be sure that the weights are correctly positioned. If they are not, overstress to the hip joint may occur. Weighted shorts such as those by Protrain have the weights placed so that their weight is in line with the thigh's center of gravity. This gives you greater safety and efficiency without any additional stress.

When doing overspeed training it is necessary to use more weight (or other modality) but not enough to disrupt running and cutting technique. For example, after one to two runs with the weighted shorts, you then take them off and run normally. You can also combine weighted shorts with Active Cords for even greater overload. After removing the shorts, you then execute the run or cutting actions with unweighted thighs and normal body weight. This type of training is most appropriate for high-level athletes and should be done only with expert supervision.

The exact number of sets, reps, and amount of weight appropriate for different periods of training has been omitted. Each athlete's physical abilities are unique and require different levels and types of training.

Basketball coaches tend to put all players through the same workout, mainly for efficiency and convenience. Maximizing each player's program and improvement requires individualized work, which takes time and effort. The burden rests on both the player's and coach's shoulders. However, only the athlete can do the work.

Remember, basketball coaches are not strength coaches. They may be great strategists and psychologists, but conditioning and preparing athletes physically for the task at hand are typically beyond most coaches, including some strength coaches. For this reason, more information on how an athlete can integrate the various types of training and establish an effective training program has been included. The bottom line: the athlete must actively be involved in the process in order to make it maximally effective.

CHAPTER 12

Integrated Training

Basketball players must work on more than improving just one quality. They must do separate training for strength, flexibility, neuromuscular coordination (technique), speed-strength (power), muscular strength, cardiovascular endurance, and so on. How to integrate these different workouts into one or more training sessions becomes very important, especially in view of the time limitations most athletes face. You should design a workout that addresses different physical qualities in a specific order.

Preferred Order for Workouts

1. Technique or Skill Learning

In order to learn or modify technique, the nervous system must be in a high-energy state. The athlete must be alert, aware, tuned into the feedback he receives, and be capable of making the changes needed to improve the actions desired. Technique comes first, before physical work.

2. Speed and Explosive Training

If no technique work is done, speed and explosiveness move to the first position. It's important to warm-up adequately, preparing the muscles for a high-intensity work. When doing both technique and speed work in the same session, technique work should be minimal. Use it mainly for reinforcement of particular skills and as a warm-up to speed and explosive training.

3. Specialized Strength Work

All exercises for strength that duplicate particular aspects of a skill technique in running and cutting *must* be done prior to other types of strength training. It takes a fresh and energetic athlete to concentrate on developing the muscular feel of a movement. Do not attempt in a fatigue state.

4. General All-Around Strength Training

General strength and conditioning (not specific to the actions involved in basketball skills) may be done when not overly fatigued. Consider doing this training after practice.

5. Muscular Endurance/Cardiovascular Endurance

An athlete may address these qualities individually or collectively. For example, there are instances when he must work on muscular endurance as needed in a typical game. Such workouts are localized to particular joint actions. This may coincidentally include cardiovascular work.

In cardiovascular work the total body is involved. Good examples are long-distance or cross-country running, cycling, and rowing. Save endurance training for the end of the session; don't ever use it as a warm-up. However, light jogging is acceptable for warm-up (and recovery).

True endurance work increases the heartbeat to a level that promotes the training effect. For relatively young (18 to 35 years old) athletes to produce an aerobic training effect, the heart rate (HR) should be in the range of 140 to 160 beats per minute (B/M). For a combination training effect of aerobic and anaerobic capabilities, the HR should be 160 to 180 B/M. To develop the anaerobic system, the HR should be in the upper range of 180 to 200 B/M.

Maintaining Speed, Strength, and Endurance

It's not necessary to continually increase strength or muscular endurance levels. This is especially true for recreational players. Maintaining strength and endurance levels is most important. An athlete who ceases workouts (and only plays) will lose some strength and endurance gains. This affects speed, quickness, and skill technique. It may also lead to injury.

Continual increases in strength or other physical qualities are not called for in-season (competitive season). In-season, maintaining and perfecting technique for accuracy and the development of strategy based on physical and technical abilities are most important. All increases in physical abilities and all technique changes should take place prior to the competitive season.

However, improved performance may be achieved by continuing speed and quickness workouts. Explosive, overspeed, resistive, and lightened cutting and running, plus the use of

heavier and lighter balls for shooting and passing and other forms of work all bring about even greater gains in speed and overall abilities. Athletes should decrease or stop strength training to prevent injury. The speed and explosive training should maintain strength levels. Maintenance work should be done only if needed.

For most recreational players, once the desired level of strength and endurance is developed, maintaining speed-strength and endurance is all that's called for. To become faster or quicker, increase levels of speed-strength. Otherwise, simply maintain current levels.

To maintain strength and endurance levels, work out one to two days per week. Do one or two sets of each exercise to maintain playing abilities. The number of repetitions varies, depending on an individual's fitness level and goals. For most players doing one set of the key special strength and endurance exercises for 10 to 20 RM is sufficient when done twice a week. Advanced players may require more work to maintain speed and quickness, especially if they're not doing speed and explosive work to maintain strength levels.

By maintaining strength and flexibility levels, older athletes maintain the ability to play the same way they did in their youth. They should increase physical abilities to play on a higher skill level.

Principles of Training

Working out means different things to different people, but how an athlete works out is critical to his development. To get the maximum results, adhere to the following principles:

Individualization: Each athlete is unique. Aside from the obvious structural differences, there are physiological differences in the muscular, circulatory, and nervous systems that require different programs. The athlete must make the final decision as to exactly which and how many exercises are needed and how many sets and reps should be done. Remember, it's possible to modify speed, strength, flexibility, and other qualities.

Gradualness: Increases in speed, flexibility, strength, resistance, repetitions, or sets should be very gradual. An athlete who's accustomed to doing 15 RM for two sets should not suddenly change to 50 to 60 repetitions, or do four sets. The body is not ready for such abrupt changes, and injuries can occur. To prevent injury and maximize results, all gains should be gradual.

Progressiveness: To show continual increases in speed, muscular strength, and endurance, progressively (but gradually) increase the amount of resistance (intensity), the number of exercises, or the total number of repetitions (volume). Doing the same number and level of exercises, sets, and reps will only maintain a fitness level.

Overload: Overload means doing more than what an athlete is accustomed to. To develop greater strength, use additional resistance. To increase flexibility, increase the range of motion. Other ways to achieve overload include increasing the rate of work, i.e., doing the exercises at a slightly faster rate of speed or in an explosive manner. These methods apply more to advanced players and should be used only after achieving base levels of strength and endurance. They include plyometrics, explosive, and other speed-strength type exercises.

Awareness: The principle of awareness is very important. Keep a workout record. Athletes should record the resistance, sets, and repetitions for each exercise, and how they feel during each exercise—keeping a log of mental and physical experiences.

Coaches should encourage athletes to be cognizant of the changes they're experiencing through training. Athletes should learn how each exercise feels and the body's response to it. Once muscle memory develops, the athlete can tell whether the exercise (or skill technique) is working, or if something is amiss. In the latter case, double-check execution, or check for another problem that may be interfering.

Consistency: Without consistency, no exercise program can produce maximum results. Exercise on a regular basis. Block off the time needed so that the exercise program becomes as important as all other activities. Once on a regular exercise program, the athlete will see the benefits quickly and be hooked into the process. This results in physical improvement, enjoyment and the kind of confidence that translates into success on and off the court.

Periodization

You now have the information needed to construct an individualized training program. The concept of periodization and cycling – how workouts should be distributed throughout the year – is fundamental to success.

In periodization, the year is divided into different periods (phases) of training. In each phase, the athlete trains in a specific manner to gain certain physical qualities or attain certain results. The resulting development enables the athlete to do the work called for in the next period of training. Positive changes from each period of training make it possible for the athlete to tackle the next phase of training, which eventually leads to the ultimate goal—improved performance on the court.

The periods of training and types of training done in each period must vary. Basketball players have multiple objectives: increasing strength, speed-strength, explosiveness, speed, coordination, etc. Training takes several directions and is divided between technique, strength, and various aspects of speed-strength (explosive) training. These objectives are accomplished while maintaining—and in some cases increasing—flexibility.

The varied demands of basketball require a range of exercises. These must be integrated in a manner that ensures results in an allocated amount of time. Training basketball players is a complex process that doesn't place emphasis on any one specific result, as typically occurs in bodybuilding and powerlifting.

The Periodization Plan

In basketball, there is one major competitive season. (Some players may play in summer leagues, but these should be considered training sessions rather than major-competitive sessions that require specialized training for preparation.) For most high school and college players, games begin in November and end in late February or early March. Team practices begin sometime in September or October, leaving only one to two months to prepare for the season. This is not the ideal situation for improving individual talents. Therefore, the onus is on the athlete to prepare during the so-called off-season.

Phase One: General Physical Preparation

The initial stage of training consists of general preparatory or general conditioning exercises to strengthen all the major muscles and joints. This should prepare athletes for the more intense training to follow. This period may also be used for rehabilitation of injuries and/or bringing lagging muscles up to par. The work in this period is general in nature. Psychological stress does not build up. The volume of work done is high, but the intensity is low. In essence, the athlete is preparing for future training.

The exact length of this phase depends on the individual's mastery of the exercises and basketball skills, his fitness level, gender, age, and so on. Younger, novice athletes should spend more time in this phase of training to increase strength and other physical qualities. For beginners, this phase can last three to four months.

A high-level player may spend two to four weeks in this period, mainly to bring the body up to a level that will enable him to train more intensely. This assumes no major loss of conditioning or skills during the off-season. For most players, this period lasts approximately six to eight weeks: March/April through May/June.

The general all-around strength program should include many varied strength exercises. For most basketball players, some of the best lower-body exercises are the heel raise, toe raise, squat, hip abduction and flexion, dead lift, good morning, and glute-ham-gastroc raise. These lower-body exercises develop the legs and muscles in the different actions that are most important in movement on the court — jumping and cutting actions.

Mid-section exercises include the 45-degree sit-up (crunch), reverse sit-up, reverse-trunk twist, back raise, back raise with a twist, and Yessis Machine sit-up. These exercises play an important role in strengthening the back to help prevent injury and developing an abdominal-muscular corset that is needed for a powerful mid-section. Development of the mid-section muscles, especially the rotational muscles, is extremely important in executing feints and different cutting actions. They are the key to enhancing a player's ability to steal the ball and/or quickly reach out to break up a play.

Upper-body exercises include the bent-over row, bench press, pull-over, full-range lateral and front-arm raises, reverse fly, biceps curl, triceps extension (palms up and palms down), supination/pronation with the strength bar, wrist curl, reverse curl, and finger exercises with the ExerRings.

These strength exercises develop the major and many of the minor muscles involved in a multitude of movements. They prepare an athlete for more intense weight-training exercises and executing basketball skills more effectively.

Start by determining strengths and weaknesses. Address weaknesses first to promote balanced development. However, do not neglect strengths; they must still be improved. Still, the amount of work done on strong points at this time should be less than that for the weaker or lagging aspects of muscle strength.

Phase Two: Specialized Physical Training

The specialized physical training period begins gradually as the general preparatory period comes to an end. This way, there is a smooth transition from general to specific training.

In specialized training, the work is specific to basketball. This means practicing specific game skills and doing specific exercises for increasing strength and speed-strength exactly as used in competition. The exercises duplicate the same motor pathway, range of motion, and type of muscular contraction, enhancing specific skill execution.

Consider these exercises, described in detail previously in this book. To improve cutting actions: hip abduction, explosive-side jumps, and single-leg side, forward, and backward jumps. For improved running speed and a quick first step: knee drive, jumps out of a squat, plyometric exercises, and quick movements out of the athletic stance.

More advanced or high-level players may have a similar program, but they usually include more sets of the explosive exercises, or use a split program to do lower-body, upper-body, and total-body explosive exercises, together with specialized strength exercises to enhance particular actions. A sample program may look like the following:

Monday and Thursday: To improve jump height: jumps out of squat, double-leg plyometric jumps, ankle jumps, depth jumps (two to three sets of 10). For cutting ability: explosive double-leg side jumps, explosive single-leg side jumps, split-squat jumps with weights in the hand or with the pull of rubber tubing, and angled-floor jumps (two to three sets of 10).

Follow explosive exercises with lower-body strength exercises. These may include squats, heel raises, standing-knee extensions, glute-ham-gastroc raises, back raises, and hip extensions.

Tuesday and Friday: To improve shooting ability: overhead medicine ball tosses relying mainly on elbow extension, use of heavier and lighter basketballs, and lying-wrist flicks. To improve passing and ballhandling: push-up jumps, chest pass with medicine balls, arm-depth jumps, side throws and catches with maximum quickness, and backward and forward medicine ball tosses.

Follow these explosive exercises with special-strength exercises. For example: overhead-triceps press, regular-grip bench press, Yessis Machine sit-ups (2 variants), Russian twist, back raises with a twist, supination-pronation, and others.

Wednesday and Saturday: Do specialty work for specific skills or physical abilities. The exact work depends on objectives and specific needs.

Most players should work on improvement of various basketball skills. For this reason, it's important to integrate training to include all of the different types of training in a timely and effective manner. At this point, it's getting closer and closer to actual competitive play. By the end of this period, the athlete should be ready to begin competition.

Phase Three: The Competitive Period

During the competitive period, training should be devoted to maintaining the physical qualities already developed. Increasing strength at this time may negatively affect technique. The key now is skill perfection and the ability to carry out these skills as part of a team concept. Look for increases in speed and quickness.

Concentrate on perfecting technique and developing the psychological and strategic aspects of the game. Work on these two aspects, along with the execution of competitive game skills. This takes place in practice, scrimmages, and competitive game play.

Because the actual minute-by-minute training workouts at this time depend to a great extent on the coach, no details are presented here. However, this is the time when basketball players should be executing many plays and drills to enhance play-making ability and carry out strategies. Working on offense and defense becomes extremely important.

Phase Four: The Post-Competitive Period

After competition, allow time to recuperate and relax—especially from a mental standpoint. The body can do physical work, but the mind must rest. Active rest is best. It's beneficial to participate in a different sport to experience physical work, enjoyment, and satisfaction. The better the athlete's skills and abilities in this secondary sport, the greater his relaxation will be. The post-competitive period lasts from two to four weeks, depending on the length of the basketball season and how long it takes the individual to *wind down*.

For those athletes who see limited playing time during the season, playing basketball in the post-competitive period can be very beneficial. Seek out opportunities to compete and put specific game skills to use. Relaxation isn't as important. This period allows for self-evaluation, and identifying strengths and weaknesses. A relatively weak athlete, who needs greater strength, may go immediately into a strength-training program. The more time spent developing strength, the more able the athlete will be to develop the speed and explosiveness needed to compete with higher-level players.

By using the schematic presented here, it's possible to achieve the highest levels of basketball play possible. Each period of training builds on the previous period of training and allows for the best performance during the competitive period. Remember, it's important to eat and supplement according to the training being done.

Avoid Early Burnout

Athletes who quickly reach top performance (within weeks or one to two months) find it almost impossible to maintain form for any appreciable length of time. This happens to many players who reach their peak early. When major competition begins, they are burned out, or have begun to stagnate. They can no longer perform at their best. The good news is that it's easy to avoid this situation.

Playing basketball on a year-round basis is not the best way to become a better player. Periodize the training. Athletes—especially young athletes—who play one sport constantly to the exclusion of all others risk burnout. Identify and participate in other activities that can enhance basketball-playing abilities. Playing in other activities is important for development of strategy and psychological qualities, but it's not the best way to develop the skills of running and cutting. Work on these separately, and then weave them into the total game presented by so many mature, high-level athletes.

Take each period of training in progression. Let the body develop in a natural manner. This promotes higher, more lasting, and better-timed peaks in performance. Equally important, the athlete will be able to start the next cycle of training fresh and healthy – a recipe for long-term, year-by-year improvement and success.

Cycling

Cycling means repeating the same action or exercise over and over. For example, the leg action in running. In essence, the athlete repeats a certain number of repetitions for a certain period of time. It also means repeating the same workout until it produces a training effect, which then leads to the desired physiological changes.

Keep in mind that the body adapts or increases in strength and other abilities only when there is repetition of a particular stimulus for a certain amount of time. The stimulus is the workout. Add resistance, but the exercises and number of sets and reps should remain basically the same.

Once a body adapts to a workout program, make a change. Don't just repeat the same exercises or routines. The body will rebel. Muscle gains will cease, and in some cases, decrease. Why? Because when a particular exercise or exercise routine is repeated over too long a period of time, there is stagnation in the nervous system. The muscles are no longer stimulated to respond. This is a catch-22 situation.

While the athlete must do exercises or an exercise routine the same way for a certain period of time to get maximum benefit, exceeding that time can bring about negative changes. At the right time, change the routine to get renewed energy of the nervous system and continued growth. The key to success is in knowing when to make the necessary changes in order to stimulate the central nervous system. This is where keeping a detailed diary of workouts is most helpful.

In general, high-level, well-conditioned, and fit basketball players must change some basic exercises (such as the squat and bench press routines) every four to five weeks. Beginners and intermediates may continue to experience gains for three to four months. There is always a wide gap between different levels of performers, and other exercises offer even greater variability. You should use a differentiated approach, geared to the individual's level of fitness and exercise and sports mastery.

When cycling, avoid five consecutive days of very intense workouts. Follow a hard day with an easy or a moderate-intensity day. Alternate in this manner during the week. When getting ready to peak or compete, it's possible to have two to three heavy days in a row, followed by some lighter days. Also, after every three weeks or so – especially if the workouts are fairly intense – insert a light to moderate workout week. This allows the body more time for full adaptation and appropriate recovery.

Many basketball players want a daily prescription in regard to what they should do for every workout. This is impossible. Each workout must be based on an individual's unique abilities. This also affects the exact amount of time spent doing each exercise or exercise program before changing.

Conclusion

While it's impossible to present a single workout to accommodate all athletes and skill levels, the general guidelines presented here are important. You can choose from many exercises and different types of programs to bring about increases in strength, speed-strength, endurance, explosiveness, etc. It's simply a matter of selecting the exercises that will enhance an individual's abilities the most, then incorporating them within the guidelines presented.

Many basketball-training programs do not follow these guidelines. Players do not train or stay in shape on a year-round basis. General conditioning and preparation often take place during a short, pre-season period. Some coaches (and players) use early games to continue preparing for more intense play. This is not the best way to become a better player.

Some basketball programs even include heavy weight training at the beginning of the season. This interferes greatly with shooting. All such work should be done well in advance of playing. The 1998-99 NBA basketball season (which, due to a lockout, did not begin until the spring of 1999 and featured no preseason games) is a glaring example of how players cannot perform well when they are out of shape at the beginning of the season. Not only did the players play poorly, they had some of their lowest shooting percentages during that season. This is what happens when an athlete isn't physically ready to play.

CHAPTER 13

Nutrition: The Foundation of Athletic Performance

To realize the greatest benefit from this (or any training) regimen, and to maximize physical performance, an athlete must eat right. This doesn't require great sacrifice; just a basic knowledge of what tastes good *and* is good fuel for the athlete's engine. There's really only one *diet* – one the athlete can stay on, enjoy, and incorporate into his lifestyle.

Throughout this chapter, recommendations and hints for athletes, coaches, and trainers are offered. Following these recommendations is a must for athletes who want to take the most out of an *Explosive Basketball* training regimen.

Embarking on an exercise or training program without the right diet is like trying to run your car without sufficient fuel or oil. Sooner or later the car will either break down or run out of gas. Think of food as an ally, not an enemy. Why? Because of the phenomenon known as *supercompensation*, which occurs in response to what is known as the *training effect*.

Supercompensation is the process by which the body stores increased amounts of energy in response to rigorous physical activity, such as the training described in this book. Over time, with the right training and diet, the body stores more and more energy during its recovery phase, enabling the athlete to train and play at a higher level. This is known as supercompensation. However, without sufficient work, the body never gets to the point of supercompensation, and simply recovers or replaces the amount of energy used during a given activity.

To improve their capabilities, athletes must exert themselves physically to experience a training effect. Supercompensation adds power, speed, strength, flexibility, endurance, and other physical qualities. It's the ticket for making progress in physical development and level of play.

For any basketball and exercise program to be successful, the athlete must eat well. This is not difficult and does not require extensive record keeping. The key is to choose a wide variety of the right kinds and amounts of foods, then eating them at the right time of day—every day.

Recommendations and Hints about Fats, Proteins, Carbohydrates, and Fiber

- Limit intake of dietary fat to about 25% to 30% of daily caloric intake. Cut down on fried foods, rich sauces, hamburgers, hot dogs, full-fat salad dressings, mayonnaise, and rich desserts.

- Use *good* oils, such as olive, canola, peanut, safflower, flaxseed, or walnut.

- Eat raw nuts (an excellent source of good fat) as a snack.

- Use butter instead of margarine. Butter is a natural product that the body can assimilate, while margarine, a trans-fatty acid, acts the same as a saturated fat and remains in the body for extended periods of time.

- Eat plenty of fish and fish oils. Fish oils help move saturated fats out of the body.

- Consume approximately one-half to one gram of protein daily for every pound of weight (approximately 30% of your daily caloric intake).

- The best sources of protein are lean meats, poultry, fish, low-fat dairy products, whole-grain cereals and breads, beans, and nuts. Fresh raw nuts and seeds are an excellent source of protein, fiber, vitamins, and minerals.

- Stick to such *complex* carbohydrates as pasta, cereals, breads, potatoes, rice, beans, fruits, and vegetables. Potato chips and candy bars don't count!

- The best sources of fiber are foods rich in high-energy carbohydrates (grains, potatoes, and beans).

- Try to get approximately 30 grams of fiber a day.

- When you make a salad, use two or three different kinds of greens, such as spinach or romaine. Add items such as celery, green, yellow or red peppers, red onions, broccoli, cauliflower, carrots, or any raw vegetable you enjoy. To liven up salads, work in foods from the grains and legumes groups. Toss some peas or beans on your greens. Olive oil and lemon juice work wonders for additional taste.

- Keep a couple of sealed plastic bags of raw cut-up veggies handy. Broccoli, carrots, zucchini, cauliflower, asparagus, green or red peppers, pea pods, fresh green beans, chickpeas, mushrooms, turnips, and tomatoes are great for snacks.

- Whole fruit is a reliable source of fiber and various vitamins and minerals. Go for the whole fruit, preferably locally grown and naturally ripened, since it is more satisfying and nutritious.

- Eat food in its natural state, and avoid processed foods. Foods eaten as close as possible to their natural state provide maximum nutrition and taste with minimum fuss or damage to the body.

- Don't rely on artificial sweeteners. These may increase feelings of hunger, as the brain interprets all sweeteners equally and triggers changes in blood sugar that mimic a reaction to sugar.

- Eat at least three times a day. The athlete's body is a finely tuned machine that needs fuel (nutrition) on a regular basis. Some athletes find that eating five to six mini-meals a day gives them more energy during the day.

- Drink lots of water. It keeps you hydrated enough to play and exercise with maximum efficiency, and it also helps the athlete's body cool itself, and get rid of its natural waste products. Drink over eight eight-ounce glasses of water a day, and don't wait until you're thirsty to drink. Your body can be short of water without your thirst letting you know about it.

- Eat food, not pills. If you eat wisely and eat a variety of foods from the different categories, you shouldn't need many additional supplements. Supplementation, as the term implies, is to supplement your diet.

- Listen to your body. Allow yourself some of your favorite foods, because many foods that you *crave* are trying to tell you something about your body's chemistry. A craving for something sweet, for example, could be a sign that your blood sugar has fallen too low. A strong urge for something salty could mean that the sweat that you are losing in your workouts has caused your body's sodium levels to dip.

Fats, Proteins, Carbohydrates, and Fiber

Even though finding and following an appropriate dietary plan is a matter of individual choice, certain basics apply to everyone – athlete or not.

Fats are calorically denser than proteins or carbohydrates. A single gram of fat contains nine calories, while a gram of protein or carbohydrate contains about four. Diets high in saturated fat, and trans fats, appear to be a risk factor for obesity, heart disease, high blood pressure, stroke, diabetes, and some forms of cancer.

A high-fat diet (especially saturated fats) typically leaves you feeling sluggish. No athlete can maximize performance given this condition. Also, dietary fat has a pronounced tendency to become body fat once consumed. This is especially true of saturated fat, found in fatty meats, full-fat dairy products, palm and coconut oil, and trans-fats (hydrogenated oils) that are found in margarine and many other products. Studies show that diets high in saturated fat tend to produce body fat in the area of the abdomen, more so than anywhere else.

Fat must *not* be eliminated or severely cut back from the diet. The body needs fat for many functions, which include assimilating fat-soluble vitamins, and manufacturing cell walls and certain essential enzymes and hormones. Fat also helps make food both more satisfying and more filling. And most importantly, fat supplies energy for continuous playing.

Proteins are very important, as they provide the basic building blocks for cellular-muscular repair and development, and they provide energy. While carbohydrates and fats supply most of the energy for muscular exertion, protein enables muscles to respond to exertion by getting firmer and stronger. It also supplies you — and your brain — with energy.

Carbohydrates are great for fast energy and in some ways the most healthful food you can eat. The more energy you have, the more capable you are going to be to have high-quality playing time and workouts. Some carbohydrates are unique; they rev-up your body's metabolic rate, even when you're just resting. Once you begin to exercise, carbohydrates really begin to kick into gear.

Fiber is the key to keeping your digestive system in shape. But fiber can also affect the shape of your body as well, mainly because fiber plays a role in excretion of dietary fat. Get enough fiber in your diet and you help sweep dietary fat through your intestines before it has a chance to be fully absorbed. This spares not only your waistline, but also your arteries and heart.

Special Nutritional Needs for a Basketball Player

Dr. Tobin Watkinson, a renowned clinical nutritionist, was interviewed about basketball-specific nutritional information for this book. He spoke about a range of issues: diet, schedule, hydration, and concentration. Dr. Watkinson emphasized that energy expenditure and nourishment for basketball playing depend to a great extent on whether the athlete is a *morning* or *night* person. Athletes must adjust their eating to meet the demands of their workout and/or competition schedules.

Carbohydrates or Fats?

At the beginning of workouts or competitive play, an athlete's energy levels are usually high. The fuel tank is full. The body soon begins to burn different fuels. Initially, it may draw upon the sugars (carbohydrates) present in its stores of glycogen. Having depleted these sugars, the body starts burning fats, which supply much more energy per unit of use than carbohydrates. As a result, athletic performance often varies from the beginning to the end of a workout.

You must train to have the body adapt to the burning of the fats. One of the most effective regimes to do this is to play or workout close to your anaerobic threshold. (In a competitive game you often go beyond this amount.) This is where you can get the greatest breakdown of fats that supply much more energy than carbs per unit of use.

You need to consume a reasonable amount of *good* fats to achieve maximum performance. By limiting the intake of fat and continually replenishing carbohydrate stores by taking in carbohydrate foods and carbohydrate-type drinks during workouts or hard play, an athlete reduces the amount of fat burned. As a result, his body may not be trained to maximally utilize the fats in the body.

Fats are not automatically burned at the most efficient rate. The athlete must train the body to adapt to the burning of fats. One of the most effective regimes is to play hard enough to be at an anaerobic threshold (and above) and to sustain it as long as possible. The burning of fats in this regime will give you much greater energy than carbohydrates, which will never be able to fuel you for a full game played at a fast pace. Keep in mind that it is only through training to utilize more fats will you be able to go longer and faster and be more explosive.

Many players who have high carbohydrate stores cannot complete a full game or play well in the second half or overtime — they literally run out of gas. Their bodies are unable to use fats, or they do not have a sufficient amount of fat for their bodies to use. Thus, you should seriously question the practice of maintaining an extremely high carbohydrate diet, or using carbohydrate drinks before and during play. By doing this, you must rely on more and more sugars for energy instead of utilizing the burning of fats to provide twice the amount of energy. If you eat a more balanced diet and train your body to utilize fats, you may find your playing (and workout) efficiency improving tremendously.

Adjust Your Eating

Each athlete has a unique body clock and must time meals and snacks accordingly to assure maximum performance.

If you are a *morning* person:

- Eat heavier starch, proteins, and vegetables for breakfast. An omelet is an excellent choice.

- Consider a mid-morning snack, including nuts and seeds (proteins which keep your sugars up, but don't give you an overabundance). It is best to have nuts raw and unsalted, unless playing in hot weather, at which time a little natural sea salt is good. Eat nuts and seeds alone. They can be digested more easily and efficiently on an empty stomach.

- Have a snack of some fruit in the afternoon.

If you are an *afternoon* or *evening* person:

- When playing in the morning, start the day with fruit and then have a mid-morning snack of some more substantial protein such as beef jerky. Evening people need to have the fruits in the morning to raise their blood sugar. Fruit, followed by a mid-morning vegetable snack, is the optimal combination.

- Nuts are an excellent afternoon snack. You need the protein to make it through to your dinner!

- Eat starches at night.

For all athletes:

- Before an afternoon workout or game, lunch is basically the same for all types of athletes. An appropriate lunch includes lots of vegetables and a little protein such as fish or chicken. Too much starch or protein is converted to sugars, making them inappropriate for lunch.

- Drinking soft drinks or alcohol is detrimental when working out or playing. Alcohol dehydrates and affects blood sugar levels. Soft drinks and sodas also impact blood sugar levels. Water is always the better choice.

Keeping Hydrated

According to Dr. Watkinson, the only thing that can totally re-hydrate the body's cells is water. Colas, soft drinks, iced tea, and sparkling mineral waters do not re-hydrate the cell the way water does. Water is the universal solvent. It enters the cell, re-hydrates it, and carries waste materials away. You will not get these results with other drinks.

There are a lot of designer waters on the market, and many are touted as re-hydration drinks. The unfortunate thing about these drinks is that they only contain one or two electrolytes, and their major ingredient is some form of sugar. It's best to have water-containing minerals such as calcium, magnesium, potassium, and sodium.

Some bottled waters are proving effective in quenching thirst; re-hydrating the body and supplying some needed elements. One such water is Oxy Water™, which has oxygen added to it. The oxygen is absorbed into the body and helps the body recover from exercise. It also oxidizes some of the waste products. Use this water as well as natural spring waters to get a full complement of needed elements.

Re-hydration is very important to a basketball player and you should drink plenty of water every day. Keep in mind that you are about 80% water and you need to have a continuous supply of good water.

Concentration

Basketball players who play a lot need to maintain their concentration throughout the game—especially near the end of the game. Concentration is basically brain chemistry—a balance between the ability to burn the fuel that you have taken in and to convert it into the appropriate brain chemistries. All the amino acids, which are the small building blocks of proteins, are the precursors to building the brain chemistries we hear so much about today. This includes serotonin, melatonin, epinephrine, and norepinephrine, as well as the other products that our brains need to be able to function as needed.

During exercise and hard play, athletes use a higher amount of brain fuels. Without replenishing these fuels, the body *stalls out*. High-demand moments, such as extremely physical games, require more brain fuel.

Emotional needs require even more nutritional support. For example, when there is a heavy emotional component (as when playing in a league or championship game), the athlete can burn up to 25 percent more calories than in regular play or practice. This is why it is so important to be well fortified nutritionally.

Athletes who consume a wide range of foods, and follow the guidelines discussed in this chapter, will be able to train and play harder and smarter than those who don't.

CHAPTER 14

Tips for Maintaining Your Training Program

Many athletes initiate an exercise program, but fail to follow through. They give up. They quit. Because of this, they rarely see all the positive results that are possible. The following are some time-tested tips that have made the difference between success and failure for many athletes.

Schedule your exercise first: This may seem heretical, as it appears to take away from your job, schoolwork, or other chores that are extremely important. However, setting time aside when you will exercise is a key element in maintaining a program. By maintaining your exercise program, your mental work will improve. This in turn makes you more efficient and productive, which enables you to get more done, and play more effectively.

Create an exercise lifestyle: Exercise and basketball should be a part of your healthy lifestyle. You must develop the habit of participation on a regular basis. Once the habit is established, it will be very difficult to break. To establish the habit, it must become a part of your normal, everyday routine.

Give your workout a fair chance: Initial exposure to any exercise or training program can be uncomfortable. This also holds true in many other areas of life. Continuing the activity and having effective instruction in its basic technique eventually leads to enjoyment and pleasure. Few activities are truly enjoyed from the very first day of participation. You learn to enjoy the activity.

Start slowly: Your body needs time to adapt in order for the gains to be seen, and most importantly, for the gains to last. Progress in any program can be fast, but any increases in volume, intensity, exercises, etc., should be slow and gradual.

Keep it individualized: The training program must be individualized to fit you. This means that you should make progress at your own rate, and that the training program must be based on your capabilities – not someone else's.

Just do it: People are great at making up excuses for why they cannot work out. They procrastinate and say they will do it at a later time. This is acceptable at times, but chronic procrastination can defeat all your good intentions. One or two skipped workouts can be quickly made up. But if you start skipping more days, it is important to figure out why and what remedial steps can be taken immediately. Procrastinating jeopardizes the success of any program, and is stressful and lowers self-esteem, further snuffing your motivation to stick with the program.

Keep a workout diary: A workout diary, either individual or in conjunction with others, can be used to evaluate your progress. The diary should show if progress is commensurate with your abilities and if any problems are developing along the way.

Forget about being perfect: Many players look for perfection. Even youngsters hesitate to undertake an activity if they do not feel they can do it well. The key here is to participate and not always be concerned with the outcome. This is especially important when beginning. Participate to get the enjoyment from the activity, in addition to achieving a certain level of fitness or playing ability.

Half a workout is better than none: If it is impossible to have a full workout, doing a partial one is still of great benefit. Flexibility is as important mentally as it is physically.

Give it six to eight weeks: It takes six to eight weeks to develop a new habit. It's also how long it takes before you experience physiological changes as a result of the exercise program. These are the long-lasting benefits that usually hook you on the activity and incline you toward greater participation.

Periodize your training: This means that your workouts change periodically, so that the one type of training you have been doing will enable you to do the next, more intense higher level of training. This cycle of periodic change (about four or more a year) not only prevents stagnation and boredom, it also enables you to make constant progress to reach your maximum potential.

Do not obsess over food: Proper nutrition is critical to peak performance. However, being obsessive in relation to the type and amount of foods you eat is detrimental to producing the best results. Avoid thinking in terms of good foods or bad foods. Instead think: variety. Most foods have some value. The main items to beware of are the saturated fats, trans-fatty acids, radiated foods, and processed foods.

Set realistic goals: When goals are realistic, they can be attained. You can then achieve the success and satisfaction needed to drive you forward.

Give it your best try: Working out requires hard work, not only in the learning process, but also when improving your abilities. When you realize that it takes hard work to receive the gains that you desire, you will be more inclined to do the work. Tell yourself it will be worth it. Remind yourself of the benefits.

Just get started: When you start effectively, you will feel like continuing. Often, the most difficult part of an exercise or training program is taking the first step. Once it is taken, you overcome much of your anxiety, and you can then really get into the training.

Draw up an agreement: Have an agreement with a fellow athlete, coach, family member, or friend. Put it in writing. By using a specific contract, the actual days on which your workouts will take place and exactly what you will be doing are spelled out. The agreement should be long-term and can include specific incentives.

It should be enjoyable: If you do not enjoy the activities in which you participate, you will quit. The key is to be active and to do exercises that can help you regardless of whether they achieve all of your goals at one time. This also applies to competitive playing. The more you enjoy it, the more inclined you will be to put in the time and effort.

Say, "Yes, I can": Research shows that affirmations, those simple positive statements that reflect your beliefs and intents, are powerful ways to keep on track or to change for the better. When you think positively, you will get positive results. The goal is to focus on the process of making positive changes and on improvements, not on perfection. The great thing about basketball and basketball training is that they are not just ends in themselves. They are a means of helping to achieve other things in life through a balanced, healthy lifestyle.

Keep an eye on the future: Focus more closely on where your basketball abilities or fitness levels will be in the next few months, or even years. If you keep your goals in mind, especially long-term goals, you will be more likely to succeed and not be set back by any minor failures. This is a great way to maintain a positive, long-range outlook.

Visualize success: When you see yourself performing well, it helps to increase self-confidence. If you can *see* it and *believe* it, it can be realized.

Dr. Michael Yessis is President of Sports Training, Inc., a diverse sports and fitness company in Escondido, CA, and Professor Emeritus at California State University, Fullerton, where he was a multi-sport specialist in biomechanics, kinesiology, and sports conditioning and training. Yessis has developed many unique, specialized strength and speed-strength (explosive) exercises and training programs. He has served as training and technique consultant to such teams and organizations as the Los Angeles Raiders and Los Angeles Rams of the National Football League, the Natadore Diving Team, and the U.S. Men's Volleyball Team. He has worked with men and women athletes from the junior high school to professional levels. Yessis is a regular contributor to *Muscle & Fitness* and *Peak Running Performance* magazines, and has appeared on numerous regional and national television programs.